*Dancing with Words*

# Dancing with Words

Helping Students
Love Language through
Authentic Vocabulary Instruction

## Judith Rowe Michaels

Princeton Day School

National Council of Teachers of English
1111 W. Kenyon Road, Urbana, Illinois 61801-1096

Staff Editor: Bonny Graham
Interior Design: Barbara Yale-Read
Cover Design: Barbara Yale-Read
Author Photo: Eileen Hohmuth-Lemonick

NCTE Stock Number: 10517-3050

© 2001 by the National Council of Teachers of English.

It is the policy of NCTE in its journals and other publications to provide a forum for the open discussion of ideas concerning the content and the teaching of English and the language arts. Publicity accorded to any particular point of view does not imply endorsement by the Executive Committee, the Board of Directors, or the membership at large, except in announcements of policy, where such endorsement is clearly specified.

**Library of Congress Cataloging-in-Publication Data**
Michaels, Judith Rowe, 1944–
    Dancing with words : helping students love language through authentic vocabulary instruction/Judith Rowe Michaels.
          p.   cm.
    Includes bibliographical references (p.   ).
    ISBN 0-8141-1051-7 (pbk.)
      1. Vocabulary—Study and teaching.  I. Title.
    LB1574.5 .M53 2001
    428.1'071'2—dc21

                                2001037003

*For Donald Roberts*
*Mentor, Friend, and Wordsmith Extraordinaire*

*Un diccionario es un sepulcro*
*o es un panal de miel cerrado?*

*[Is a dictionary a sepulchre*
*or a sealed honeycomb?]*

Pablo Neruda
*The Book of Questions*

# Contents

# *Foreword*

*T*he history and present state of language teaching in the English classroom provide a classic study of lip service. Enlightened teachers across our land admit, indeed proclaim, that language is the most important hallmark of our humanness, and that a focus on language, pure or applied, can vitalize the English classroom, for both the teacher and the taught. Most English teachers accept as the curricular model the tripod, triad, triumvirate, or trinity of literature, composition, and language, and perceive that since language is the medium for the other two parts, it is central to the school as well as to the human experience.

Yet surveys show that language study has come to occupy only about 10 percent of the English curriculum, falling far behind programs in composition, literature, and even speech. Too often, that 10 percent of study devoted to language learning is restricted to grammatical analysis and isolated usage drills. Students write S, V, DO, and IO above the subject, verb, direct object, and indirect object of a sentence and are initiated into the intricacies of *lie* and *lay, less* and *fewer,* and *compose* and *comprise.* (Do you, O fellow inmate in the house of correction, really understand that last distinction?)

The study of grammar and usage can be fascinating, but presenting language skills as a lineup of "thou shalt's" and adversarial exercises explains why, when meeting English teachers, people respond with the likes of "Gee, I'd better watch my grammar," or "English was my worst subject." Do we really want to be viewed primarily as linguistic sheriffs who organize

posses to hunt down and string up language offenders who have the temer-
ity or ignorance to float their *hopefully*s, split their infinitives, and dangle
their participles in public? Do we want to be the objects of such zingers as:

St. Peter hears a knocking at the Gates of Heaven and calls out, "Who's
there?"

A voice answers, "It is I."

And St. Peter sighs, "Oh no, not another English teacher!"

Judith Rowe Michaels is a teacher who encourages her students to hang
out with words. Like Samuel Johnson, she is never "so lost in lexicography
as ever to forget that words are the daughters of earth." She knows there is
more to language study than has been dreamt of in our previous philoso-
phies. She knows that language is like the air we breathe. It's invisible, it's
all around us, we can't get along without it, yet we take it for granted. But
when we step back and truly listen to the sounds that escape from our
mouths and spring from our electronic keyboards, we are in for a lifetime of
joy. And it *is* a lifetime because language, unlike mathematics and science,
is something we get better and better at during our lives.

She knows that language play in the classroom is naturally transmuted
into language power in the student. She knows that as students come to see
language as an activity not apart from them but a part of them, they will use
language more competently, confidently, creatively, intentionally—and
playfully.

She knows that by serving as the chief means we have for exchanging
our emotions, thoughts, and ideas, words are the foundation of our society.
She knows that words are the tools we have for living and striving together.
She knows that words and people are inextricably bound together through
history.

Has it ever struck you how human words are?

Like people, words are born, grow up, get married, have children, and
even die. They may be very old, like *man* and *wife* and *home.* They may be
very young, like *veggies* and *househusband.* They may be newly born and
struggling to live, as *netiquette, gangsta rap,* and *political correctness.* Or they
may repose in the tomb of history, as *leechcraft,* the Anglo-Saxon word for
the practice of medicine, and *murfles,* a long defunct word for freckles or
pimples.

Our lives are filled with people and words, and in both cases we are
bound to be impressed with their vast numbers and infinite variety. Some

words, such as *OK,* are famous all over the world. Others, such as *foozle* (a bungling golf stroke) and *groak* (to stare at other people's food, hoping they will offer you some), are scarcely known even at home.

Some words we will probably never meet, such as *schizocarps* (pinwheels that grow on maple trees) and *vomer* (the slender bone separating the nostrils), and others are with us every day of our lives, such as *I, the, and, to,* and *of,* the five most frequently used English words.

As with people, words have all sorts of shapes, sizes, backgrounds, and personalities. They may be very large, such as *pneumonoultramicroscopic-silicovolcaniosis,* a 45-letter hippopotomonstrosesquipedalian word for black lung disease. They may be very small, such as *a* and *I.*

Some words are multinational in heritage, as *remacadamize,* which is Latin, Celtic, Hebrew, and Greek in parentage. Some come of Old English stock, as *sun* and *moon* and *grass* and *goodness.* Some have a distinctly continental flavor—*kindergarten, lingerie, spaghetti.* Others are unmistakably American—*stunt* and *baseball.*

Words, like people, go up and down in the world. Some are born into low station and move up in life. With the passing of time, they may acquire *prestige* (which used to mean "trickery") and *glamour* (which began life as a synonym for "grammar"). Others slide downhill in reputation, such as *homely* (which originally meant "homelike; good around the home"), *awful* ("awe-inspiring"), and *idiot* ("one who did not hold public office").

Words such as *remunerative, encomium,* and *perspicacious* are so dignified that they can intimidate us, while others, such as *booze, burp,* and *blubber,* are markedly inelegant in character. Some words, such as *ecdysiast,* H. L. Mencken's Greek-derived name for a stripteaser, love to put on fancy airs; others, such as *vidiot* and *netiquette,* are winkingly playful. Certain words strike us as beautiful, such as *luminous* and *gossamer,* others as rather ugly—*guzzle* and *scrod;* some as quiet—*dawn* and *dusk,* others as noisy—*thunder* and *crash.*

That words and people so resemble each other should come as no surprise. Words and people were created at the same time: an article in *Scientific American* ("We Were Not Alone," January 2000) explains that many early hominid species, some of them coexisting, preceded the tenure of *Homo sapiens.* Today we take for granted that we are the only hominid on Earth, yet for at least four million years many hominid species shared the planet, including *Homo habilis, Homo erectus,* and, of course, *Homo neanderthalensis.*

What made us different? What allowed us to survive? The answer is on the tip of our tongues. While some of these other species possessed the physical apparatus for speech, only with *Homo sapiens* did speech tremble into birth. The development of language made us human, and our humanity ensured the survival of language. We human beings have always possessed language because before language found a home in the mouths of hominids, it was not fully language and we were not fully human. Language and humans together created history, and together we career through history. Humankind not only possesses language, but we also *are* language.

**Richard Lederer**

# Acknowledgments

*Many thanks to Princeton Day School for helping me create the position of artist-in-residence, which allowed me some time for working on this book, and to my students, whose responses to language inspired me to spend more time exploring it, both in class and out. To my parents' love of music, reading aloud, and letter writing I owe much of my initial interest in language. And later, my husband's fascination with wordplay and his daily immersion in poetry—from Wallace Stevens's and John Ashbery's to my own—encouraged me to go on dancing with words.*

# Permissions

WE GRATEFULLY ACKNOWLEDGE THE PUBLISHERS WHO GENEROUSLY GAVE US PERMISSION TO REPRODUCE THE FOLLOWING MATERIALS:

LI-YOUNG LEE: "Persimmons," copyright © 1986, by Li-Young Lee. Reprinted from ROSE, by Li-Young Lee, with the permission of BOA Editions, Ltd.

"Teachers' Convention" by Judy Michaels, *Nimrod International Journal, Y2k.connecting,* Vol. 42(2), Spring/Summer 1999.

NAOMI SHIHAB NYE: "One Boy Told Me," copyright © 1998, by Naomi Shihab Nye. Reprinted from FUEL by Naomi Shihab Nye, with the permission of BOA Editions, Ltd.

"since feeling is first." Copyright 1926, 1954, © 1991 by the Trustees for the E. E. Cummings Trust. Copyright © 1985 by George James Firmage, from COMPLETE POEMS: 1904–1962 by E. E. Cummings, edited by George J. Firmage. Used by permission of Liveright Publishing Corporation.

"Neruda." Copyright © 1993 by Wanda Coleman. Reprinted from *Hand Dance* with the permission of Black Sparrow Press.

Excerpt from "The Snows of Kilimanjaro." Reprinted with permission of Scribner, a Division of Simon & Schuster, from THE SHORT STORIES OF ERNEST HEMINGWAY. Copyright 1936 by Ernest Hemingway. Copyright renewed © 1964 by Mary Hemingway.

"I the Survivor" from "Poems 1913–1956" by Bertolt Brecht. English language translation © John Willett, reproduced by permission.

# Chapter 1

# *Persimmons and Times When*

*I* know that readers tend to miss the epigraph completely in their rush to get at the meat of a book, and the preface often doesn't stand a chance either. So in this prefatory chapter, I want to begin by rereading my epigraph from Pablo Neruda's *Book of Questions*—"Is a dictionary a sepulchre / or a sealed honeycomb?"—because it sets the tone and hints at the method of *Dancing with Words*, which is to admit right from the start that word is still out in cognitive research circles on exactly how we acquire a vocabulary. So why not, having posed the unanswerable question, relax and start dancing?[1]

Robert Coles, in a preface I actually did read because he always tells me something I didn't know I needed to hear, recalls how his fifth-grade teacher would sometimes announce a "times when" period,

> in which we were invited, any of us, to stand up and tell a story about something that had happened to us. We loved those occasions, because we were free at last of rote memorization, of unquestioning compliance with rules and mandates and arbitrary customs (as in spelling!) of various kinds. Rather, we were allowed—better, encouraged—to let our minds find their own directions, have their own say in their own way.

Coles goes on to remember how a classmate once read aloud a poem she'd written one "time when" she'd tried to catch a robin and he "short-flied" across her lawn. "The poem asked why—why the distrust, when no harm was meant, rather a gesture of friendliness. 'But nature said no'—and here I am, a half-century later, remembering those four words, the simple, direct beauty of them, their various implications."[2]

As I read Coles's words, I realized that my book is trying to help teachers create memories like that one—of times when certain words made an imperishable impression on the senses, the mind, the heart. This idea is the theme of *Dancing with Words*. Each chapter can be read by itself, and the chapters could probably be read in any order since each offers a different approach to helping students engage with words—from moving to them, to chanting them, to letting the power of free association combine them, to exploring personal connections they hold, to creating fiction and poetry with them, to getting news from them in a city newspaper. But the chapters are, actually, arranged in a kind of order: we move from collecting and examining individual words, to bringing them to life with our bodies and voices, to juxtaposing them in phrases and sentences—poetry and narrative—through both free association and the laws of syntax and grammar, to letting them help us enter the outside world, and, finally, to recognizing their mastery over us as we probe the inner world of our solitary imagination. Classroom exercises appear in each chapter, and sometimes even in chapter notes, but they are not meant to be prescriptive. Rather, readers should feel free to adapt the ideas to their own teaching lives and students.

Perhaps because I am a poet as well as a high school English teacher, and much of my work in schools involves reading and creating poetry, I have a bias against vocabulary workbooks and exercises that require looking up long lists of words in the dictionary. I love browsing in dictionaries, whether sepulchres or honeycombs, and set aside class time for students to do so, but I want their encounters with words to be meaningful in the best senses of the word—in the sense Coles has in mind when he praises his fifth-grade teacher for letting "our minds find their own direction, have their own say in their own way." And I don't want to make too many distinctions between the mind of a ten-year-old and a sixteen-year-old. A twelfth grader should have the opportunity to engage with the word *persimmon,* even though it will not appear on the College Boards, in something of the same spirit of wonder she might have felt back in sixth grade when her teacher brought in a persimmon to class—or with the complexity and richness that we encounter in Li-Young Lee's memorable poem:[3]

### Persimmons

*In sixth grade Mrs. Walker*
*slapped the back of my head*
*and made me stand in the corner*
*for not knowing the difference*
*between* persimmon *and* precision.
*How to choose*

*persimmons. This is precision.*
*Ripe ones are soft and brown-spotted.*
*Sniff the bottoms. The sweet one*
*will be fragrant. How to eat:*
*put the knife away, lay down newspaper.*
*Peel the skin tenderly, not to tear the meat.*
*Chew the skin, suck it,*
*and swallow. Now, eat*
*the meat of the fruit,*
*so sweet,*
*all of it, to the heart.*

*Donna undresses, her stomach is white.*
*In the yard, dewy and shivering*
*with crickets, we lie naked,*
*face-up, face-down.*
*I teach her Chinese.*
*Crickets:* chiu chiu. *Dew: I've forgotten.*
*Naked: I've forgotten.*
Ni, wo : *you and me.*
*I part her legs,*
*remember to tell her*
*she is beautiful as the moon.*

*Other words*
*that got me into trouble were*
fight *and* fright, wren *and* yarn.
*Fight was what I did when I was frightened,*
*fright was what I felt when I was fighting.*
*Wrens are small, plain birds,*
*yarn is what one knits with.*
*Wrens are soft as yarn.*
*My mother made birds out of yarn.*
*I loved to watch her tie the stuff;*
*a bird, a rabbit, a wee man.*

*Mrs. Walker brought a persimmon to class*
*and cut it up*
*so everyone could taste*
*a* Chinese apple. *Knowing*
*it wasn't ripe or sweet, I didn't eat*
*but watched the other faces.*

*My mother said every persimmon has a sun*
*inside, something golden, glowing,*
*warm as my face.*

*Once, in the cellar, I found two wrapped in newspaper,*
*forgotten and not yet ripe.*
*I took them and set both on my bedroom windowsill,*
*where each morning a cardinal*
*sang.* The sun, the sun.

*Finally, understanding*
*he was going blind,*
*my father sat up all one night*
*waiting for a song, a ghost.*
*I gave him the persimmons,*
*swelled, heavy as sadness,*
*and sweet as love.*

*This year, in the muddy lighting*
*of my parents' cellar, I rummaged, looking*
*for something I lost.*
*My father sits on the tired, wooden stairs,*
*black cane between his knees,*
*hand over hand, gripping the handle.*

*He's so happy that I've come home.*
*I ask how his eyes are, a stupid question.*
*All gone, he answers.*

*Under some blankets, I find a box.*
*Inside the box I find three scrolls.*
*I sit beside him and untie*
*three paintings by my father:*
*Hibiscus leaf and a white flower.*
*Two cats preening.*
*Two persimmons, so full they want to drip from the cloth.*

*He raises both hands to touch the cloth,*
*asks, Which is this?*

This is persimmons, Father.

Oh, the feel of the wolftail on the silk,
the strength, the tense
precision in the wrist.
I painted them hundreds of times
eyes closed. These I painted blind.
Some things never leave a person:
scent of the hair of one you love,
the texture of persimmons,
in your palm, the ripe weight.

## Notes

1. Pablo Neruda, # LXVII, *The Book of Questions*, trans. William O'Daly (Port Townsend, WA: Copper Canyon Press, 1991), 67. This bilingual edition of a collection of poems Neruda completed just months before his death—seventy-four short poems posing 316 unanswerable questions, sometimes haunting, sometimes comic, sometimes both at once—has many virtues, one of which is that it transforms teacher and students alike into questioners, seekers of truths that resist the kind of reasoning generally valued in school. The poems also offer splendid examples of the power of simple language to create images that invite exploration of the connections between concrete and abstract, between the tangible and the spiritual. When I introduced these poems to various classes during one of my visits to a wealthy suburban high school, I was interested to see that the "slow" English classes responded much more immediately and imaginatively than the AP sections, who dismissed the excerpts as "not poems at all" and Neruda's questions as "dumb." Generally, all one needs to do is hand out a sheet of thirty couplets, let every student read one aloud, asking them to leave a little silence between each one, and then go around once more to hear which couplet "spoke" to which student. There's no need to probe for reasons, though sometimes a student will offer one. A question that a lot of people choose: "And does the father who lives in your dreams / die again when you awaken?"

It's also interesting to have students make two lists, one of Neruda's concrete nouns and one of his abstract nouns, then make their own lists of concrete and abstract nouns, and finally try writing a few unanswerable questions, combining words from both lists. Because Neruda's text appears in both Spanish and English, students who know Spanish can do this in Spanish. In fact, it's a fruitful exercise to try in any language.

2. Robert Coles, Foreword, in *Learning by Heart: Contemporary American Poetry about School,* ed. Maggie Anderson and David Hassler (Iowa City: University of Iowa Press, 1999).

3. Li-Young Lee, "Persimmons," in *Rose: Poems* (Rochester, NY: BOA Editions, 1986).

# Chapter 2

# The Resonating Word

Words, their taste and heft, their play and range, their trickiness and power, have been mistrusted for a long time. By Plato, when poets wielded them. By indigenous peoples and immigrants, when lawmakers wielded them. And by the young, when adults used too many of them. Today in most circles a love of words is still distrusted. Language is merely the bailiwick of writers.

*Bailiwick:* Where does it live in the body? Voice teachers say that a whole universe of sounds lives within each of us, and that with training and greater openness to possibility we could learn to produce them all—including sounds we might consider "primitive," foreign, embarrassing, or acceptable only from the throats of opera singers. But one of the best ways to "learn" a word is to locate its syllables, its music, within us. Why does *sneer* register more immediately and viscerally than *satirize?* Look in the mirror and say it, slowly, tasting each individual sound. It contorts our face. The "sn" bares our teeth a little; it's perilously close to "snarl." Adding the short "e" lifts the upper lip unattractively toward the nose, makes the eyes squinch up, wrinkles the forehead, and creates a sound we associate with expressions of dislike or evil ("yecch," "leer"). And the "r" hints at an animal growl from between clenched teeth. By contrast, *bailiwick* has a slightly comic set of sounds, much less threatening, though perhaps equally memorable—the light "li" and the kiss of the "w" soften the sneer of the short "i" and the final hardness of "k." *Sneer* and *bailiwick:* These two words alone evoke a whole symphony of sounds, actions, and feelings.

   *Bailiwick, scalyprick, whale lick, cowlick, cow chip, lickety-split, lackluster, split rail, bailout, jump bail, bait and switch, witch hazel, wishy-washy, wisenheimer, wiseacre* (Middle Dutch *wijssager*—prophet), *wiseass* (slang—sometimes vulgar). One word leads to another. They are tricksters, shape-shifters, in their associative powers of sound and image. When allowed to associate freely and figuratively in poetry, songs, or the visionary writing of mystics, they can persuade us against, or beyond, our reason—for good or ill. According to Saint John, life itself began with the Word, the divine truth that was "with God," that "was God." To Plato, Aristotle, and Zeno, this Logos was the rational principle that governed the universe. Zeno, the founder of Stoicism, linked two meanings of *logos*—reason and speech—to argue that this creative force gave human beings, made in God's image, the power of logical thought and discourse, thereby setting them above all other forms of life. Later, a person's *word* came to mean his honor, his authenticity, his trustworthiness. "She's a woman of her word." "I give you my word of honor." But, says Trickster, whose word? Whose honor?

   Before written language, words were the domain of the bard, the griot, the shaman—the dream keepers, list makers, healers, spellbinders. According to Norse mythology, Odin, king of the gods, risked his life to drink from the well of poetry because, he said, such power over words conferred power over life. He shared it with those gods and men who he felt were most capable of wielding it.

   Who would not want such power? The power of trickster and healer, dreamer and ruler, the power of a god? And miraculously, a deep well of words is available to our senses and imagination, from birth onward. Young children drink from it without hesitation. Visiting a kindergarten class on a winter morning after an ice storm, I write the word *icicle* on the board, and we say it together till we start getting silly—icicle, icicle, tricycle, micecycle, ice cream, ice dream, mice scream. . . .

   This playful experimentation is the miraculous process of acquiring language, and with it the capacity to reflect, to imagine, to remember, that creates world and self. Given enough encouragement, we continue to grow as our experience with language deepens. But today in high schools throughout the country, this miraculous process has been allowed to die an unnatural death. "Vocabulary" is, for most adolescents and their teachers, the rote memorization of a few hundred abstract, Latinate polysyllables in preparation for a once- or twice-in-a-lifetime test.

What does it mean to "know" a word? To "learn" the language that is one's own? Listen to Pablo Neruda on the subject:

> [I]t's the words that sing, they soar and descend. . . . I bow to them. . . . I love them, I cling to them, I run them down, I bite into them, I melt them down. . . . I love words so much. . . . The unexpected ones. . . . The ones I wait for greedily or stalk until, suddenly, they drop. . . . Vowels I love. . . . They glitter like colored stones, they leap like silver fish, they are foam, thread, metal, dew. . . . I run after certain words. . . . They are so beautiful that I want to fit them all into my poem. . . . I catch them in midflight, as they buzz past, I trap them, clean them, peel them, I set myself in front of the dish, they have a crystalline texture to me, vibrant, ivory, vegetable, oily. . . . I shake them, I drink them, I gulp them down, I mash them, I garnish them, I let them go. . . . I leave them in my poem like stalactites, like slivers of polished wood, like coals, pickings from a shipwreck, gifts from the waves. . . . Everything exists in the word. . . . An idea goes through a complete change because one word shifted its place, or because another settled down like a spoiled little thing inside a phrase that was not expecting her but obeys her. . . . They have shadow, transparence, weight, feathers, hair, and everything they gathered from so much rolling down the river, from so much wandering from country to country, from being roots so long. . . . They are very ancient and very new. . . . They live in the bier, hidden away, and in the budding flower.[1]

I know that as a writer and teacher, or simply as someone who is trying to live in the world as fully as possible, I want not only to "master" a word—be mistress of its music and range of meanings—but also to be mastered by it. To find it lodged not only in my memory but in my body, heart, and spirit. To feel it, as Keats said of poetry, on the pulses.

So I propose that we help high school students rediscover the miracle of language. Not by quizzing them each Friday on SAT word lists, but by creating an atmosphere of playful curiosity and creativity that will allow discoveries to occur naturally each day—the way young children learn language—and by building in the time to make students aware of what they're discovering. In my K–12 work as a poet in the schools and an arts coordinator, I've found that many of the ways in which young children learn and grow are applicable to my own high school English students; the older students simply have to be liberated from their self-consciousness and their narrow concepts of what is adult and what is "vocabulary." There are ways to do this, many of which serve the additional purpose of appealing to a range of "intelligences," to use Howard Gardner's term—the kinetic, the spatial, the inter- and intrapersonal, the musical.

How to make the time for such a yearlong process? I suspect many of us have found that less is sometimes more when it comes to covering curriculum. "You never really finish anything in life, and while that's humbling, and frustrating, it's all right." I read this recently in Kathleen Norris's *The Cloister Walk;* she is quoting a friend who was educated by Benedictines. Norris, a midwestern poet, teacher, and memoirist who became an oblate in the Benedictine order, has a lot to say about "liturgical or poetic time"—time that is "oriented toward process rather than productivity." I keep coming back to her insistence on "the contemplative potential of the reading process" that "respects the power of words to resonate with the full range of human experience."[2]

Suppose I have to skip "teaching" a scene from *Othello* because a preliminary free-association exercise on the word *jealousy* has escalated into a free-for-all discussion—of its connotations, its behavior in our mouths and on our faces, its gestures, its derivation, its place in the Old Testament, how it differs from envy, what imagery it calls up in our writing, and what we can remember about our own experiences coping with it. I hadn't planned most of this. But as I listen, I'm beginning to see the payoff: how each student is finding his or her own way into the word, even into the fascination of word study, and how, through this preliminary exploration, we can each bring our own personal knowledge of jealousy to our reading of the play—which will help us enter into Iago's and Othello's destructive passions. Already students are curious about these characters' jealousy, about "the green-eyed monster" and its ravages. Their empathy and curiosity will help us over the hurdles of unfamiliar language, syntax, history, and geography and will certainly result in more powerful discussions, stagings, papers, and projects. So maybe it'll be okay to skimp on analyzing a scene or two. We'll bag the part about the Turkish fleet; we'll skim a soliloquy. And next year I'll build the jealousy class into my plan book.

A colleague objected, "But they already *know* the word *jealousy*. You can't count that as vocabulary." Which made me realize how the label "vocabulary" has narrowed our view of language study. How unnatural to pretend that the only language of relevance to adolescents is a few hundred mostly Latinate words primarily used for making distinctions and analyses and (sometimes) for weighing down a speech or essay to the point of pomposity—*ameliorate, fallacious, mitigate, paucity, inadvertent.* I have nothing against Latin or abstraction; my grandfather was a fine Latin teacher, and I took all the Latin I could in high school and in college. That language has its own music: just listen to the beauty and power of the Gettysburg Address—*dedicate, consecrate, devotion.* But where in the lists of Princeton Review is any enthusiasm for the crazy word hoard that is English—all those words so rich in sound and connotation that stir the senses and thus the memory, that galvanize the body into action, that stimulate creative thinking and writing and talk, and that have, often, a fascinating history? Words that make us realize what a hodgepodge our language is—like *skulk* and *slump, masquerade* and *blather, galaxy* and *double-talk, pretzel* and *spook.* And—one I just learned yesterday—*dead-cat bounce:* a temporary recovery in stock prices after a steep decline, often resulting from the purchase of securities that have been sold short.

Surely vocabulary is more than learning "difficult" words. It's about how the meaning of a word can expand over the centuries from literal to figurative, from concrete to abstract, accreting new layers, perhaps shedding some of the old ones. It's about how the archaic or obsolete meaning may continue to live on, a shadow or secret skeleton, contributing an almost invisible shading, a subliminal coloration, to the contemporary usage. How did the abstract noun *hypochondria*—excessive worry about one's health—grow from the Greek *hypo* (under, below) and *chondros* (the cartilage of the breastbone)? Because the chondros was believed to be the seat of melancholy (Greek *melano*—black—and *chol*—bile). What might such expansion suggest about the society and time (mid-1500s) in which this new meaning emerged? Did it reflect a growing leisure class? A humanistic interest in personal health, in ownership of one's body? A new birth of medical knowledge? Whatever the cause, I will now check out my breastbone for melancholy before I think about phoning the doctor.

Why are no two words, even synonyms, exact equivalents? Who was it who said the difference between the right word and the nearly right word is that between the lightning bug and the lightning? Why is translating a poem from a foreign language so frustrating? What is the difference in music and connotation between *phony* and *fake*? Can a cliché ever be granted new life?

Who decides when an expression has become a cliché? What is an idiom and why should we find it hard to write idiomatically in our own language? What determines when a new word enters the dictionary? What does Pablo Neruda mean by asking whether a dictionary "is a sepulchre or a sealed honeycomb?"[3] Where do new words come from, anyway? (The street, the real estate office, the press, the medical profession, the government, the entertainment industry. . . .) What's the difference between slang and jargon? How did the invention of the telegraph help shape the language of Lincoln's Gettysburg Address?[4] In which decade did *babysitter* enter the language, and why then? Is there really such a thing as a perfectly objective definition? Can we make room in our lives for columnist Dave Barry's definition of a sommelier: "a wine steward, the dignified person who . . . says 'Excellent choice, sir,' when you point to French writing that, translated, says 'Sales Tax Included'?" Or for his discovery that "'weasel' is a funny word. You can improve the humor of almost any situation by injecting a weasel into it."[5] What words do you find funny for no good reason? And why are some words that seem so "easy" sometimes so complicated— words like *community, real, fair, beauty, friend, bitch, work, self, true?*

## Notes

1. Pablo Neruda, *Memoirs*, trans. Hardie St. Martin (New York: Farrar, Straus and Giroux, 1977), 53–54. Reading this autobiography by Chile's Nobel Prize– winning poet and political activist makes clear how lyrical language can serve the needs of people of every class and culture but particularly those who are poor and have no formal education. It invites one to question Auden's famous dictum that "poetry makes nothing happen," and it reveals how the Spanish Civil War transformed a poet from a private person into one who wanted his words to serve the people, "to dry the sweat of its vast sorrows and give it a weapon in its struggle for bread." Excerpts from this memoir could inspire students with a new appreciation for the power of language and serve as an introduction to some of Neruda's stirring love sonnets, which are especially effective in a bilingual edition.

2. Kathleen Norris, *The Cloister Walk* (New York: Riverhead Books, 1997), xix. This is a remarkable book, a series of personal meditations, poetic and witty and practical and spiritual, on everything from community, feminism, marriage, and celibacy to language, religion, suffering, death, and the nature of time. It is very much about learning and teaching, and is worth taking time to

read slowly—savoring, copying bits into journals and letters—whether you can read it only for five minutes before going to bed or choose the greater continuity afforded by summer vacation. It has been the subject of book discussions on a California Web site for teachers.

3. Neruda, *The Book of Questions* (see note 1, chap. 1).

4. Gary Wills, *Lincoln at Gettysburg: The Words That Remade America* (New York: Simon & Schuster, 1992), 169–75. Gary Wills manages to be both scholarly and lively in his study of the origin and circumstances of this famous speech. In arguing that Lincoln with his few words effected "an intellectual revolution," Wills contends that the speech's urgency derived not from a superabundance of short Anglo-Saxon words but from its "internal 'wiring' and workability." Lincoln "was not addressing an agrarian future but a mechanical one. His speech is economical, taut, interconnected." Wills notes that

> Lincoln, who considered language the world's great invention, welcomed a cognate invention, telegraphy. He used the telegraph to keep up with his generals. . . .Lincoln spent long hours in the telegraph center at the War Department, and was impatient with the fumbling and imprecise language still being used on this instrument, which demands clarity as well as concision. . . . Lincoln's telegraphic eloquence has a monosyllabic and staccato beat. . . . The unwillingness to waste words shows up in the Address's telegraphic quality— the omission of most coupling words. . . . The language is itself made strenuous, its musculature easily traced, so even the grammar becomes a form of rhetoric.

The Address is worth studying not only in history classes but also in English classes, and anyone interested in language will find much to think about in Wills's book.

5. Dave Barry, "Daze of Wine and Roses," in *Dave Barry's Greatest Hits* (New York: Ballantine, 1988), 20. And Dave Barry and Jeff MacNelly, "Introducing: Mr. Humor Person," in *Dave Barry Talks Back* (New York: Crown, 1991), 6.

# Chapter 3

# First Day

**First Day**

We size each other up, and I would like
to birth each one, shiny, red, and freshly fourteen,
from a rib, from a ventricle, from an armpit—nothing
too sexy, this is school, but intimate,
an indelible connection that we'll remember
when rain turns this gray room grayer and I call it
silver, autumnal, they will think Nah,
it's fucking up football but—fondly?—Yeah,
autumnal's not bad, that's just the way the old
woman is, and they'll think back to how warm it was
in the good old right ventricle, and I'll have
some built-in credibility without being
the Home Mom they have to break on a wheel
every couple of days.
                      And I won't teach them
hygiene and sex and vegetables
and I won't just be the Great Dispenser of
Grades, but this mythic guardian whose genes
are theirs so we recognize the same thresholds,

*shapeshifters, dragons in black holes,*
*and know why we have to start journeys*
*to save something that's dying in a distant wood—*
*it's in the blood, we gotta go there—*
*and when it's time to start singing on the rocks,*
*or let ourselves be wrecked for a while,*
*well, our eyes and skins turned out to be different*
*but we all came from one place, and when it rains*
*so everything's real* autumnal, *we don't*
*forget, we kinda want to get back there.*[1]

*E*ach of us has his or her own language. But in any classroom, a common language starts to grow right from the first day. I know my own vocabulary to be thoroughly Romantic—*silver, autumnal*—rooted in my favorite English poets and New England Transcendentalists. But it's been beefed up by thirty years of exposure to students and a growing fascination with contemporary theater and poetry, the multicultural and feminist movements, jazz, the visual arts, newspapers, dance and film and music criticism, gay rights activism, Zen Buddhism, dictionaries of slang, children's literature, and Dave Barry columns.

To excite students about language and help them discover and develop their own, a teacher needs to be ready to say, even in midsentence, "I wonder what this word means. Does anybody here know? Okay, let's look it up." And, maybe more important, we need to be on the alert for interesting—or even just characteristic—words and phrases used by our students: "'Cut the fluff?' Kelly, I love it!" And up it goes on the board—*Cut the fluff*—with her initials under it, as a valuable reminder of how to edit. By the end of the year, most of us will have gotten better at fluff cutting, but we'll also have one more example of what writers mean by "voice." And we'll have strengthened our sense of ourselves as a community—by adding one more phrase to our common language.

Handing out the assignment sheets on this opening day, I stumble over Tom's long, outstretched legs—these desks are really too small for growing teens—and I realize I'll probably go on stumbling over them all year. "Oh, sorry," I tell him. A few weeks later, he's written a poem about his feet, which he describes as "Clydesdales." With his permission, I read the poem aloud, asking everyone to listen for words that we should put in our notebooks. The horsewoman in the class picks this one and explains that Clydesdales are strong, high-stepping horses with long hair along the backs of their legs. She giggles. And then I suddenly remember noticing the word in my little paperback slang dictionary (*21st Century Dictionary of Slang*), which I keep a copy of in the classroom.[2] I look it up: "(Teen & College): attractive guy, derived from handsome horse breed." We all giggle, and both definitions go into our notebooks.

I'm having students keep their own word lists all year long. In the past, we did this for a month in the spring during our poetry-writing unit, which I always kicked off by showing my own writing notebook full of words, clippings, and rough drafts. Then I began to experiment with taking time after the daily five-minute period for free reading to share interesting words and phrases we were encountering in our various books. The results were so good—a couple of students even chose to browse in a dictionary during some of their reading time—that I resolved to build this activity in every day.

Starting the class with free reading had already helped focus the students on language. In a five-minute spurt, they're more likely to notice individual words than in a forty-five-minute homework assignment. It also made them more aware of the different reading tastes of their peers. On the second day of the school year, when each person had brought in a book from home or chosen one from the classroom library (which I stock with a range of genres, collections of photographs, and various schools' literary magazines), we take time to hear volunteers read aloud a paragraph from their choices. "How many of you think you might want to look into this book, based on what Kate read to us?" I count the hands—"Hmm . . . a lot of girls. Is there such a thing as a girls' book? A guys' book? Who in here likes sci fi? War novels? Who thinks, "I probably wouldn't like . . .?" Gradually, as the year goes on, we find ourselves breaking down certain stereotypes and expanding our own repertoires. (I read *Childhood's End* and like it.) Every month or so I ask my classes to put together a list of recommendations, each of us annotating a few new finds and suggesting which classmates might want to try our titles. Students keep reading cards on file with me—title, author, rating, and brief annotations—and we discuss books in conferences and freewrites.

Given this structure, it's easy to heighten student awareness of language. From the very first week, the notebook—wordbank, wordpool, wordhoard— becomes a collaborative effort. We each collect our own words—from class reading and discussions, eavesdropping, graffiti, song lyrics, recipes, newspaper and magazine articles, ads, readings in other courses, and our own areas of expertise. But we also copy in the words we share after the five-minute reading periods.

It's important that I read and fill my notebook right along with the students. If a few days go by in which I've broken this rule in order to organize my lesson plan better, I notice them starting to lose interest. Sometimes I'll begin the sharing process myself: "Today I'm reading a poetry collection by a friend, Renée Ashley—*The Various Reasons of Light*.[3] I love this phrase right here, 'the urgent furnace of her life,' partly because of the way the sounds in *urgent* and *furnace* go together—the push of the repetition makes it *sound* urgent—but also because it gets me thinking about my own life. How is life a furnace?" I write the phrase on the board, and we copy it into our notebooks, underlining the repeated sounds.

And then, after a long pause, someone says *furnace* makes him think of the Bible and the three men cast into the fiery furnace who don't burn up— and maybe life is a sort of miracle like that, because it's so dangerous and we're living so hard. Somebody else says life is a flame, but sooner or later your flame gets put out.

"But not if you believe in an afterlife," a third kid objects.

"Yeah, but you can't prove it," says my resident skeptic. "Religion is just a crutch."

And I see we could be in for a full-period discussion, so I say, "We could argue this one all year, but we need to move on. But for now, notice how far the image of the furnace took us? How much can be evoked by that single image—how many associations it brings up? And we haven't even asked yet about what the *fuel* is—and how it's acquired. As part of your homework tonight, let's come up with two more images for life—that is, a concrete noun, something you could draw, with an adjective attached if you want. Let's write for five minutes on each image in order to explore how it works. We'll put these new possibilities up on the wall tomorrow. Over the centuries, people have found this is a very powerful and creative way to think— through images and associations."

And then Julie reads a passage from her book, Barbara Kingsolver's *Pigs in Heaven*, about how the Cherokee Nation is trying to reclaim the American

Indian child, Turtle, from her adoptive mother, and how, during an interview with a native lawyer, the mother is trying to keep birds from eating the apricots off the tree in her front yard because Turtle "likes apricots more than anything living or dead, and she's the kind of kid that just doesn't ask for much." As long as the boom box the mother has strung up in the tree continues to play her lover's demo rock band tape, the birds stay out of the tree, but at the end of the interview with the lawyer, the tape also ends, and the birds fly back and "reclaim" the tree. "'One by one the birds emerge from the desert and come back to claim their tree,'" Julie reads. "That's a neat symbol." So we put into our notebook, "birds reclaim apricot tree—will Cherokees reclaim Turtle?"

Next day Jon asks to read aloud from *All Quiet on the Western Front*. His passage is about how the character's "inner camera focused," so we jot down the phrase and discuss what one's inner camera might be. Parker says it's "his photographic memory." Someone else says that it just means "seeing everything really clearly and sharply." And then a third student suggests it's "seeing with the mind's eye—like with his imagination."

I'm still engaged with Renée's poems, so I bring up another of her phrases—"a half-assed arabesque." Ilona, who we discover has been studying ballet for many years, says she can demonstrate an arabesque better than describe one, so she does, extending her body slowly and beautifully, flowerlike. Then Jon offers to do it "half-assed." "Be sure you're using only one half!" his friend Patrick warns him. And I think *yes*, these two guys are going to be very useful when it comes to staging scenes from Salinger and Shakespeare and Fugard. And thank God for Ilona, since this winter we'll be prepping to see a performance of the ballet *Billy the Kid.*

The third day someone reads a sentence that contains the word *woozy.*

"Tired?" Dmitri suggests.

"No, dizzy," Jen corrects him.

"It's a funny-sounding word. Where do you suppose it came from?" I ask, and call for a volunteer to look it up in the classroom dictionary.

At Parents Night, I'll encourage everyone to make sure their kids have a good hardcover dictionary at home—the school makes some secondhand ones available—and in class I'll photocopy an individual page from my own or put it on the overhead projector to see whether each student knows how to read and interpret an entry. But during these brief language sessions, we rely on my *Random House Webster's College Dictionary.*[4]

"Woozy," reads Jennifer—"1. stupidly confused; muddled. 2. physically unsettled, as with dizziness, faintness, or slight nausea. 3. drunken. [1895–1900, *Amer.*; perh. short for boozy-woozy.]"

I suggest looking up *booze*—"which sounds sort of slangy, doesn't it?" But it turns out to have come into the language in the 1600s, deriving from the Middle English *bous* (strong drink) and the Middle Dutch *busen* (to drink to excess). Our acquaintance with derivations is expanding.

As the year goes on, I ask students to carry tiny pocket notebooks or else a few file cards with them whenever possible to record windfalls that come at odd moments; they can later transfer these into their main word collection. I tell them that I do this myself, and that I often write down whole phrases or sentences—quotations from movies, songs, dreams, conversations, even ideas for poems and articles. I read to them from Anne Lamott's lively book on writing, *Bird by Bird*, about the virtues of these little file cards:

> I have index cards and pens all over the house. . . . I carry one with me in my back pocket when I take my dog for a walk. In fact, I carry it folded lengthwise, if you need to know, so that, God forbid, I won't look bulky. You may want to consider doing the same. I don't even know you, but I bet you have enough on your mind without having to worry about whether or not you look bulky. . . . I . . . head out, knowing that if I have an idea, or see something lovely or strange or for any reason worth remembering, I will be able to jot down a couple of words to remind me of it. . . . I might be walking along the salt marsh, or out at Phoenix Lake, or in the express line at Safeway, and suddenly I hear something wonderful that makes me want to smile or snap my fingers—as if it has just come back to me—and I take out my index card and scribble it down. . . . I have an index card here on which is written, "Six years later, the memory of the raw fish cubes continued to haunt her," which I thought might make a great transitional line. But I have so far not found a place for it. You are welcome to use it if you can. [5]

What will we do with the words we collect? I remember a student conference with a girl who'd written a prosy, predictable poem about losing her boyfriend—"suddenly the sun started to dim. . . / You leave me there, standing in your shadow, / alone, as I hear your footsteps moving / further

and further away." Neither of us had liked it much. Now Jen showed me a
new version that she said she was very proud of. It ended:

> *My eyes began to swell as salty drops of water*
> *fell upon my white tank top*
> *creating a sheer appearance in which*
> *everyone could clearly see right through my body*
> *and into my broken heart.*
> *The shattered pieces left marks upon everyone whom*
> *I've touched.*

"So how did you find your way into this new language?" I asked, admiring some of the images.

"I looked back in my word lists, and that got me going," Jen said. "It was
the lists you had us make of nouns and verbs from different categories—you
know, weather, buildings, food, but especially the one on clothing. That led
me into the tank top image, and I was able to picture myself the day he and
I split up. I remembered exactly what I was wearing and thought about what
I must have looked like, and it all got much more personal and detailed. I
didn't have to explain how I was feeling."

In fact, she was so pleased with the revision that when visiting poet
Naomi Shihab Nye came to class and asked to hear our poems, she was the
first to volunteer. Naomi liked the detail about the tank top made transpar-
ent by tears.

Of course, one could argue that becoming a collector is a good thing in
itself. Parents generally encourage their children to build collections,
whether of butterflies or baseball cards, on the theory that the child gains
some confidence and sense of individuality along with the new expertise in
entomology or the history of the Yankees. I collected praying mantis cocoons for a brief period in fifth grade—not for class but just because I was
fascinated by the way the brown-gray foamy little bundles were camou-
flaged in the weeds. I loved the triumph of spotting one woven to a twig in
the underbrush of our back lot. I did read articles about these insects, but
not imaginatively enough to realize what would happen when the twenty
cocoons hatched in my mother's china bowl on the dining room buffet. Nor
was I inspired to become an entomologist or even a writer on insect life. But
I learned some new language—that one of the plural forms of mantis was
*mantid*, for example, and that mantid were *predacious*, the female mantis

actually devouring the male. Which led me to connect *pray* with *prey*. Later, when I read about Clytemnestra, I pictured her with long green feelers.

I also enjoyed telling my parents and my girlfriends about mantid. And I now realize that doing this reinforced what I had learned from observation and reading. So it seems important to make opportunities for students to share their word collections. There are many ways to do this. Let them pair up and read one another's notebooks, and ask them to steal the words they like best from their partners' lists. Or put them in small groups and, after they read the notebooks, ask each student to act out a word that appeals to him or her for the others to guess. Or let them collaborate on creating a story or dialogue using words from the group's lists.

I think these methods are all more productive than handing out standardized word lists and tests. Students' lives are sufficiently haunted by tests already; mine assure me that the typical vocabulary quiz is "the kiss of death" and stops them from wanting to collect more words. While testing is one way to convey that "this material matters," reliance on it leads kids to believe that there are no *other* reasons why language is important—and that "vocabulary" is a kind of artificial activity relevant only to test days. Richard Lewis, a poet-in-the-schools of New York and Japan, is eloquent on the need for incorporating "the triad of learning, so that mind, body, and feeling are one entity," and "not separating learning from the taproots of curiosity and imagination." He emphasizes the role of imagination, how without it, "we don't know ourselves or each other," and how school, despite its "concern for the mechanics of literacy . . . too frequently makes the recipients of its teachings incapable of relating to what is alive and meaningful in themselves." Lewis goes on to quote Alfred North Whitehead on how students learn: "You must not divide the seamless coat of learning. What education has to impart is an *intimate* sense for the power of ideas, for the beauty of ideas, and for the structure of ideas, together with a particular body of knowledge which has *peculiar reference to the life of the being possessing it"* [italics mine].[6]

One of my favorite language activities, because it involves "the triad of mind, body, and feeling," is what I call "performing the mural." In this activity, the whole class gets to read and speak as individuals, yet in the process it is creating a communal piece. Everyone chooses a different color crayon or marker and, on a huge piece of colored paper I put up on the wall, they enter words from their collections that they particularly like for sound or image or associations. I encourage them to include foreign words, slang, and words from their reading in other courses. Last spring's first mural included: *tsunami, bitchin, Rasputin, resplendent, careworn, guts, meander, i'iwi, papier-mâché flowers, leer, dreadlocks, solipsistic, brillo, sultry, watermelon girl, nor'easter, bouffant, hive, waddle, malamute, diablo, pimp strut, fish tank, painstakingly, wigwam, coif, cirrus, opaque, monsoon, yacht, saunter, apocalypse, insinuate, melba, haughty, psychological smile, spinach, effectual, medulla oblongata, iglesia, philanthropist, névé.*

When everyone's put up a few words, we all gather around the mural. "We're going to give a reading," I tell them. "The rules are: Take initiative to read anyone's word you want, in a voice and pace that suits it, but try not to overlap with someone else's voice. Be sensitive with your eyes and ears and 'feelers' to who's about to read—but if you do overlap, keep going, don't worry. It's fine if a word gets read more than once—we'll get to know them better if we keep hearing them in different juxtapositions. Listen to the overall effect, and if you think we've heard too many in the same rhythms or textures or pace—too much legato (sustained smoothness) or too much staccato (short, abrupt sounds), try to vary the pattern. Or if you notice an interesting combination of two words, be ready to say one right after somebody else says the other one. Listen to the overall production, but enjoy each solo."

After the initial self-consciousness, students begin to listen. Gradually we hear ourselves extending the sounds of *insinuate, sultry, leer, melba, careworn,* and *watermelon* and punctuating them with almost jazzy, percussive repetitions of *guts, coif, pimp strut, yacht.* We begin to notice and enjoy the way different voices color the performance—soprano, alto, tenor, bass. We even get brave enough to experiment with exaggerating certain sounds, with whispering, with varying the pitch for different syllables of a word. *Fish* (high) *tank* (low). I try a downward glissando on *careworn.*

There turns out to be something almost mystical about this experience—something I can't account for. Even the skeptics are drawn in. Each of us becomes attuned to the others. Our focus is a wonderful combination of relaxed and intense—like the "flow" experienced during the height of the creative process. Voices arise suddenly, mysteriously, from behind us, from right next to us, from the other side of the room. The richness of the language—not just English but the human language of soft and hard, sweet and harsh, abrupt and flowing—emerges from the page, from our throats, into our bodies and imaginations.

As I listen to the sounds of these words connecting, not in conventional syntax but more like individual notes of music falling unpredictably on the ear and inviting it to create some new kind of sense, I remember the distinction that poet Kenneth Koch makes between ordinary language—"a vast, reasonable, practical enterprise, with vocabulary and syntax and grammar"—and poetic language, "in which the sound of the words is raised to an importance equal to that of their meaning. . . . Poets think of how they want something to sound as much as they think of what they want to say, and in fact it's often impossible to distinguish one from the other." [7]

As we listen to the words on the mural come alive, we aren't just hearing denotations. The effect is more like a description I read recently in David Abram's book about language and nature, *The Spell of the Sensuous*:[8]

> Active, living speech is . . . a gesture, a vocal gesticulation wherein the meaning is inseparable from the sound, the shape, and the rhythm of the words. Communicative meaning is always, in its depths, affective; it remains rooted in the sensual dimension of experience, born of the body's native capacity to resonate with other bodies and with the landscape as a whole. . . . [M]eaning sprouts in the very depths of the sensory world, in the heat of meeting, encounter, participation.

After this kind of sensuous participation in one another's words, students start asking questions: "What's a *coif* ?" "Yeah, and who put up *pimp strut*? Where'd you find that?"

Happily, no one volunteers to demonstrate it.

## Notes

1. Judy Michaels, "First Day," *English Journal* 88 (July 1999): 110.

2. Princeton Language Institute, ed., *21st Century Dictionary of Slang* (New York: Dell, 1994). This handy paperback organizes its lists by subjects such as advertising, crime and law, ecology, fashion, technology, etc. Its "Note on Usage" warns that the meanings of slang terms can be "subtle and implications depend on circumstances. . . . Know your audience." It excludes terms "that describe the sex act, parts of the human anatomy, or any that refer to sexual preference, ethnic background, or size."

3. Renée Ashley, #5, "The Various Reasons of Light," in *The Various Reasons of Light: Poems* (New York: Avocet Press, 1998), 16.

4. *Random House Webster's College Dictionary* (New York: Random House, 1997). This is the dictionary I turn to most often for recent words, meanings, and usages. I also like the clarity of the definitions and the typeface, and I enjoy browsing with students in the prefatory essay "Defining Our Language for the 21st Century," which includes lists of words according to the decade in which they entered the language.

5. Anne Lamott, *Bird by Bird: Some Instructions on Writing and Life* (New York: Anchor, 1994), 133–42. The novelist and memoirist offers a witty, anecdotal discussion of the writing life and craft. Her delight in words is apparent throughout, and her advice is often relevant to high school writers and their teachers. She quotes an old Mel Brooks routine in which the therapist tells the patient, "Listen to your broccoli, and your broccoli will tell you how to eat it." Or, as Lamott explains, "You get your intuition back when you make space for it. . . . Rationality squeezes out much that is rich and juicy and fascinating." Excerpts from this book have helped my student writers relax sufficiently to discover fresh juxtapositions of words through freewriting and free association.

6. Richard Lewis, *Living by Wonder: Writings on the Imaginative Life of Childhood* (New York: Parabola Books, 1998), 44–45, 84. Lewis has founded the Touchstone Center, a New York–based source for workshops and books that offer children (and adults) various entries into their creative imaginations through speculating about the mysteries of nature, time, the body, and the mind by means of the visual arts, dance and theater, poetry, myth, and music. His work grows directly from his own practice as an artist in the schools and as a parent.

7. Kenneth Koch, *Making Your Own Days* (New York: Scribner, 1998), 21. This book by the well-known New York City poet who popularized the poet-in-the-schools programs through his books on teaching poetry—*Wishes, Lies and Dreams* and *Rose, Where Did You Get That Red?*, among others—is subtitled *The Pleasures of Reading and Writing Poetry*. It explores the idea that poetry is a separate language, one in which music and sound are as important as syntax or meaning, and shows how confusion during the reading of a poem can eventually lead to truly experiencing the poem. This is a good corrective for those of us—teachers and students alike—who are prone to reading a poem

in class and then demanding immediate "right answers" to its mysteries. The book includes a rich collection of poems from a variety of languages and cultures, with Koch's brief commentary on each. It is helpful to hear a poet respond to Marianne Moore's "To a Steam Roller" in this casual, open-ended way:

> The subject matter, the whole idea of talking so seriously to a steamroller, is funny. A reader may suppose, too, on the basis of Moore's other poems, that the "steamroller" probably represents a person Moore doesn't like, perhaps a literary critic. In which case, who knows what the "butterfly" may represent—perhaps the steamroller's mistress or wife. The identity of these two is not a "hidden meaning" but simply something else to think about—the steamroller and the butterfly are enough.

As a struggling poet trying to make myself clear, I find it very discouraging to be accused of deliberately planting a "hidden meaning" in my reader's path, and as a struggling teacher of poetry, I try hard to ban this popular term from the classroom. "Something else to think about" is a nicely untechnical and unthreatening phrase.

8. David Abram, *The Spell of the Sensuous: Perception and Language in a More-Than-Human World* (New York: Pantheon Books, 1996), 74–75. This is a book about language, but it's also about breaking down boundaries—between man and nature, philosophy and psychology, poetry and ecology. Abram, who is a scholar of philosophy as well as a student of the relationships between magicians and the natural elements, explores the nature of perception and, in particular, the power of language to enhance or stifle "the reciprocity between our senses and the sensuous earth." To quote the book jacket, "Animal tracks, word magic, the speech of stones, the power of letters, and the taste of the wind all figure prominently in this astonishing and intensely ethical work."

# Chapter 4

# The Pebbles and Marbles Game, or Self and Community

*I*t's mid-June, the last day of school. Return of exams and closure. My ninth graders sit with me in a circle on the floor, taking turns saying what they remember best from the past year together.

"The Poetry Café," says one kid, who had predicted this event would be a total bust, totally humiliating and boring.

"Parker acting drunk when he played Cassio in the *Othello* scenes," says someone else. "Parker, you were great!"

"The pebbles and marbles game we did the very first day of class," says Emelia. Some murmurs. "Oh . . . yeah." It seems like a very long time ago.

Actually, it was in my eleventh-grade class where this game led us to a discussion of the words and concepts of *self* and *community*. Ninth graders are generally too anxious and self-conscious on their first day of high school to think beyond, "God, that guy with the dark curly hair and the incredible tan is so cool. And whatever I say, I'm going to sound like a jerk." With them I play pebble and marble mainly in order to help us all see we've got some interesting experiences and expertise among us that, as a group, we'll be able to draw on this year. And that we each are bringing some worries and anticipations with us—that no one is as cool as he seems.

We sit on the floor in a circle, my bag of pebbles and my box of marbles in the center.

We close our eyes, and I lead the class in a short breathing exercise to calm them down and get them focused. Then, keeping their eyes closed, every student takes a marble from the box and a pebble from the bag. As they hold one in each hand, I ask them to focus on the difference in shape and texture. Then I ask them to think about a strength they can bring to the group—not necessarily a strength related to English, simply a quality that might be good for the group. I also ask them to think about some worry or anxiety they've brought with them to school; it doesn't have to be connected with school, but it does have to be something they're willing to tell us. "I know it's early in the year for risk taking, so this doesn't have to be some-thing very, very private, but it should be something you really are worried about. As you listen to your classmates' voices, think about what it will feel like to be part of this group, with its strengths and worries. Which strengths do you find yourself especially admiring, and which worries can you relate to?" Momentary panic. Then for a while the room is quiet. After a few minutes, we go around the circle, and as we name a strength, we put in the marble; as we tell about an anxiety, we put in the pebble. Gradually the two piles grow in the center of our circle. The exercise works best if we all keep our eyes closed the whole time so that we aren't aware of how we look—of who's blushing, who's nudging whom. Hearing the disembodied voices is somehow more powerful and holds our interest better than if we could see each speaker. I participate; in fact, I usually go first to break the ice.

Finally, we open our eyes, and I direct everyone's gaze toward the accumulated marbles and pebbles in the center. "Any thoughts about these?"

It was in the junior class that someone said, "These are us. How strange. Each of us is there, in both those little heaps. And every time we have a discussion, all these things will be feeding it somehow. I guess that's how you become a group. You kind of know where each person is coming from. You have some things in common."

I had just been reading a book called *Words and Values*, by Peggy Rosenthal, about certain words that over the past forty years or so have taken on new associations.[1] Among these words were *self* and *community*. Rosenthal argues that *self*, as a positive concept, as something more than a reflexive pronoun or an element to be subjected to the will of God and King, didn't really come into the English language till the nineteenth century, whereas *community* has long been a positive term, compared, say, to *state* or *society*, and more recently has become a "feel good" word, employed to conceal many kinds of political, religious, and aesthetic agendas. Given my student's observation, the history and connotations of these two words seemed like a promising place to begin our word study. I also thought about a fascinating book by Raymond Williams, *Keywords: A Vocabulary of Culture and Society*, that explores in considerable depth such words as *individual, identity, soul, psyche, ego, personality,* and *character,* as well as *common, commune, communism, society, city, state, clique.*[2]

These word clusters were a good way to explore class dynamics, but it also later occurred to me that much of the literature studied in English courses, both the "classics" and the growing multicultural canon, reflects conflict between the individual and the community: *Antigone, The Catcher in the Rye, Their Eyes Were Watching God, The Outsiders, Twelfth Night, To Kill a Mockingbird, The House on Mango Street, Huckleberry Finn,* the poetry of Whitman and Dickinson—and on and on.

So the next day I write on the board *self* and *community*. "Look around you at the individuals in this circle," I tell the juniors. "Would you say that the circle is a community? Is a community the same thing as a group? No, let's not talk yet. Just put these two words in your notebook, and we'll freewrite on each one for five minutes. No, you won't be graded. You won't have to read aloud. I'm going to write, too. We can make lists to start with, or write about what associations each word holds for us. Or some experiences we've had that relate to one or both of them. Or try to define each word and guess where it came from.

"Let's start by closing our eyes a minute and just saying each word to ourselves a few times to find out what its music is—where it takes place in our mouths. Really taste it. Meditate a little on the sounds. *Ss-el-l-ff. Commun-i-ty.*"

As I do this, I notice the initial hiss of *self*—snakelike warning, confidential whisper, pent-up steam emerging from between the teeth and tongue—followed by the backward movement of tongue and teeth for the *e,* then the tongue upward for the prolonged liquid *l* and the firm, aggressive thrust, almost pout, of the lips for the soft cutoff of the *f.* As I repeat *community,* I feel how the "com" makes an enclosure, coming from the *c* in the back of the throat, opening with the *o,* and bringing the lips together on the *m;* the sensation reminds me that the prefix *com* in Latin means "together" or "with." Since this is the first day of class, I tell the kids these things I'm feeling and thinking. Later, they'll be able to talk about their own discoveries with one another.

"Now write both words in the air with your finger—no, keep your eyes closed. What do the letters feel like? What does your mind's eye see in the air? Start small, with just your fingers and hand. . . . Now let your whole arm swing into it, and write very large. Imagine your whole body dancing the letters. . . . Suppose they were graffiti on a wall? Suppose they were huge letters of fire—some kind of message—maybe a warning? An invitation?" As I write in the air, I feel the two extremes of the *l* and the *f,* the soaring, stretching loop and the downward loop. And all the curves—the hills or waves—of *community*'s *m*'s and *n,* the pauses for the little percussive movements of dotting the *i* and crossing the *t.* I'm registering in my body the difference between the monosyllabic Anglo-Saxon and the polysyllabic Latin. As well as the poetry of *self*'s brief singleness or oneness (which E. E. Cummings characterized as the "l[oneliness]" of a single *leaf* but also as "there's nothing as something as one") versus the winding, curving length of *community*'s enclosure.

Admittedly, this is not a very scientific approach to language. But Peter Elbow, in *Writing without Teachers*, says that

> Meaning in ordinary language—English, for example—is midway on a continuum between meaning in dreams and meaning in mathematics. . . . (. . . the meaning-building rules for dreams are the rules of "resemblance" and "association." But everything resembles everything else to some extent, and anything is liable to be associated somehow with anything else. Thus anything can mean anything.)
>
> [In mathematics,] people have gone to the trouble to nail down the rules for building meaning into symbols. . . . In mathematics there *are* mistakes, and any argument about what something means or whether there is a mistake can be settled without doubt or ambiguity. (Perhaps there are exceptions in some advanced mathematical research.)[3]

To the word *self* I and some of my students may, on any given day, bring to discussion sudden recollections of E. E. Cummings's numerous poems about one, someone, anyone, "oneliness." We may also think of Dr. Seuss's celebrations of individuality—or, indeed, when we hear *community,* we may think of his celebrations of togetherness. Someone studying European history may think of the Paris Commune or of communism. Elbow writes that

> the individual user of ordinary language is like the dreamer. He is apt to build in any old meaning to any old word. Everybody has just as many connotations and associations to a word as he does to an image. . . . [N]otice that words *do* in fact end up meaning anything as they move through time and across mountain ranges. "Down" used to mean "hill" ("dune"), but because people said "down hill" a lot ("off-dune"), and because they were lazy ("adown"), finally hill means down. Philology, it has been said, is a study in which consonants count for very little and vowels for nothing at all.[4]

Which reminds me of David Abram's explanation of the original Semitic "alephbeth," invented around 1500 B.C.E.: It "established a character, or letter, for each of the consonants of the language. The vowels, the sounded breath that must be added to the written consonants in order to make them come alive and to speak, had to be chosen by the reader, who would vary the sounded breath according to the written context."[5]

Traditional vocabulary workbooks and word lists for standardized tests assume that dictionaries are the authority on meaning—and that there is a correct meaning dwelling in every word, which individual students must master in order to communicate clearly with their community. And in one sense, of course, this is true. How can you have a community in which, as Humpty Dumpty said, a word "means just what I choose it to mean— neither more nor less"? A community in which *glory* means "a nice knock-down argument," for example. But there are times when, for many of us, a nice argument—one that we win—*is* glorious. Just as there are doubtless occasions when sex has felt like Orwell's "doing your duty to the Party." Elbow pushes us to think harder about the nature of meaning:

> Strictly speaking, words cannot *contain* meaning. Only people have meaning. Words can only have meaning *attributed to them by people.* The listener can never get any meaning out of a word that he didn't put in. Language can only consist of a set of directions for building meanings *out of one's own head*. Though the listener's knowledge seems new, it is also not new: the meaning may be thought of as

*structures* he never had in his head before, but *he* had to build these new structures out of ingredients *he* already had. The speaker's words were a set of directions for assembling this already-present material.[6]

Of course, Elbow recognizes that

> the mathematics-like force for order is just as strong [as the dream force]. That is, though words in ordinary language *can* mean anything, they only do mean what the speech community lets them mean at that moment. . . . These rules for building meaning may be thought to be written down in dictionaries. But dictionaries are only records of yesterday's rules, and today's may be somewhat differ-ent. And dictionaries don't tell all the meanings that speakers send to each other in words.

Moreover, to further complicate the dynamism between dream force and math force—which, says Elbow, is the history of meaning in language—"there are many overlapping speech communities for each individual—building up to the largest one: all speakers of, say, English." Or, say, Span-ish, in San Antonio. The smaller communities—one's circle of friends or one's own family or one's office mates—"are not as strongly stabilizing as the larger speech community. . . . And so, in fact, the smaller communities turn out to act as forces for *fluidity* upon larger communities."[7]

Of course, a smaller community may have more power, at least in particular settings. In "my" classroom, I am the only adult—a minority of one; but as teacher, as a more experienced writer and reader, and as grade giver, my rules may take on more force, during classes and on student papers, than the larger language community of the adolescent majority. On the other hand, if I keep myself open to the various languages of the stu-dents—the sports lingo, the bits of street slang, the computer terms, the speech conventions of ethnicities different from mine—and stay alert for all those creative student usages which, like Humpty Dumpty's, bully the dictionary into submission, I can become a more fluid force in the class-room language community.

Elbow offers a helpful description of the individual's process of making meaning—which he calls "gestalt-making" and compares to the shifting

interpretations possible when the viewer looks at one of those line drawings
that can suggest both a vase and the profiles of two people facing each
other:

> But it doesn't look like both at once. It jumps and looks very differ-
> ent as you change gestalts. Here is a visual field, then, that invites
> two conflicting gestalts. . . . The act of seeing seems inherently an
> act of construction that makes wholes out of fragments. The same
> thing goes on in sound: we hear as melody and shape what are
> disconnected sounds.
>
> The same thing goes on in finding meaning in a set of words.
> Because words are full of redundancy and ambiguity (which turns
> out to be efficient in a communicating medium) an utterance tends
> to consist, as it were, of seventeen words, each capable of as many
> as three or four meanings. In listening, you've got to hold up in the
> air countless possible meanings of parts—and even meanings of the
> whole—and then find the whole that makes the most sense. Read-
> ing or listening is like seeing: you have to build the gestalt that
> makes the most coherence out of an ambiguous semantic field.[8]

"So what are you discovering about self and community?" I ask the
students, having written along with them for ten minutes or so.

"Well, I was thinking about why I don't like it when some adult gets up
at assembly and talks about *the school community*," Sam says. "It feels so
fake. Like they're just saying it to get us to do what they want."

"Yeah," Barb agrees. "I don't feel really close to more than maybe twenty
or thirty kids in the school. I mean, it's not that I dislike a lot of the people
here, but I certainly don't feel like they're part of *my* community. I don't
want someone else telling me who my community is. I guess that's part of
being myself—I know who I am partly by who I choose as my friends."

"There're a lot of communities here, if you think about it—I don't mean
cliques, like in junior high, but, like, interest groups. And they overlap,
which is cool. Like, I'm part of the theater crowd but a lot of my friends are
my hockey teammates, and I've gotten close to some of the debate kids
when we did the Model UN trip."

"But when we have those town meetings in the theater, don't you kind of
feel that there are certain kids who say things that make you so mad you
can't believe they're part of the school? I mean, where are they *coming* from?"

"But they have the right to say anything they believe in. It's freedom of speech. Or states' rights. I guess you could say the school's like the federal government—yuck! It's better than *that*—and each of us has certain freedoms to be who we are. And try to change stuff we don't like. Like remember when Tanji spoke up about how the theater program needed to be more open to black kids—how they didn't even think about trying out for the plays? And I kind of thought, So who's stopping you? But then she said stuff that made me really think about it. And I thought, she's right. So that's an example of people feeling left out of a community they have the right to be part of."

"You know, hearing you say 'the black kids' that way—like we're all alike—that really bothers me. I didn't agree with Tanji. I don't want special favors. Being on stage—that's not who I am anyway. We don't all feel the same way."

"Okay, okay. So I didn't mean it that way—it just came out wrong. But it's an issue in the real world, too—blacks not getting roles. Look at the stereotypes on TV and in movies. And how many black movie directors are there out there? Suppose you did want to be an actor? Suppose that was who you are? You couldn't get to be your*self* as easily as a white guy could in this society that's supposed to be so free."

"It's like gays not being able to be themselves, really, unless they're out."

"That stinks, you know? Why do you have to compare blacks and gays? I can't stand it when people do that."

"And besides, you don't have to be out to know who you are."

"No, but how can you have, like, a gay community if only a couple of ' gays are out?"

"Well, if I were gay, I wouldn't want to be lumped with other gays just because—I mean, I might not even like some of them. Who needs a community, anyway?"

"Well, not to change the subject or anything, but I wrote about—you know how we were reading about Buddhism in Religious Civ. and how you're supposed to empty yourself and not even think about being an individual self—which seems to go against most of what everybody's saying here. Like on your college essays and your whole application deal, you know they say you have to make yourself stand out in the crowd, show how you're this special individual with these unique talents. And I like to think of myself as unique, but when I get depressed, that's when I think I'm not special at all, just part of the crowd. And then sometimes I think, well, I *like* being part of my crowd. But that's 'cause they like me for who I am. I fit in."

"Well, I don't think of having a community here. My community's my family. Clubs and teams and stuff, that's just stuff I do."

"The first word I thought of was *community service,* and how some people just do it to make themselves look good for college or because we have to, and I thought about how even though I liked working at the nursing home last year, I still didn't feel like I was part of all those people—like they were my community. I felt sorry for them, and a couple of them were really fun to talk to, but I don't want to ever be in that situation. I want always to be an outsider there."

"Yeah, I had to visit my granmom when she broke her hip and was in the rehab center, and I felt the same way. I'd shoot myself if I had to actually live there for long. I guess I can't imagine myself that old and helpless. It wouldn't be me any more."

"Well, what I wrote about kind of fits in with that. I got going on empathy, and how you can't have a *real* community without it, and how it's really, like, remember in *To Kill a Mockingbird* where he says you have to be able to walk in somebody else's shoes? So you're leaving your own self behind and going into somebody else's, or maybe taking yourself with you, so you come out sort of bigger—like a bigger self."

Everyone seems caught up in this discussion, and I hesitate to interrupt them, but—"Did anybody get to thinking about any of the 'self' words—you know, all those words that start with *self?*" I ask them.

"Yeah, actually I made a list—like *self-conscious, selfish, selfless, self-centered, self-control, self-confident, self-sacrifice, self-reliant, self-motivated,*" Matt says.

I write them on the board and open the dictionary: "Look, there's a whole section of them down at the bottom here, plus three whole pages." And I add to the list: *self-pity, self-effacing, self-denial, self-image, self-explanatory, self-defense,* and *self-evident* (as in "We hold these truths to be . . .").

"Then there's the whole self-help movement. Does that expression feel any different to you than, say, self-reliance?"

"Yeah. . . ." Janet wrestles with this. "'Self-reliance' sounds good—like being able to survive in the wilderness or being able to fix your own car. 'Self-help' always sounds kind of . . . well, silly, like trendy, like. . . ."

"Like pop psychology," says one of the top chemistry students. "You know, for people who need someone to simplify everything for them, even when it's really complex."

"Did anybody notice there's a special section for self-help books in the *New York Times Book Review* list of best-sellers?" I ask. "Take a look at it some time—stuff on everything from dieting, to organizing your time, to doing your taxes, to knowing what colors look best on you, to investing in the stock market."

"There's always a big section in every bookstore for books like that," Janet agrees. "What really gets me is seeing stuff on dieting"—Janet, admittedly, is a runner and all muscle—"right next to how to grieve. These should all be things you know how to do naturally—by instinct—what to eat so your body feels good, when you need to cry and when you're ready to stop. It's like nobody trusts themselves, they have to buy the book."

"It's really weird," Matt says. "*Self-help* is one of those words that tries to sound good—like making you think you're doing it yourself—but Janet's right, it's just the *opposite* of self-reliance if you need a book to tell you how to feel or what to wear."

"If we were all Buddhists, we wouldn't be worrying about any of this. It's all our Western capitalist emphasis on the self—all our consumerism. Like those ads about 'buy this—you owe it to yourself.' We really don't have selves anymore," Janet says.

"But you don't have to do what the ads tell you to. That's just dumb. I don't buy stuff unless I want it. How can you be original if you're a Buddhist and just lose your identity? How would any great paintings get painted? And inventions."

"Yeah, and how about love? If we all emptied ourselves of desire, that would mean we wouldn't have personalities, and you can't fall in love with somebody who doesn't have a personality. Do you just have to love everybody the same—like some of those weird utopias?"

"I don't know how we got on to all this religious stuff," says one of our economists. "You've got to have individuals so you can have competition so you can have progress, and you've got to have communities because, well, the buyers and sellers are a community, they depend on each other, like stockholders' investments support the corporations, and this way they get dividends. The art and religion are just sidelines. They're nice to have, but a country could do without them."

"I suppose *you'd* say we could do without love, too, as long as the stock market kept rising. That's really what community is all about—when two people fall in love and you get beyond two little egotistical selves. All this self—it's just ego."

"It sounds like you're realizing how complicated these words are." I want to refocus a little. "You know, I was just reading a book that looks in-depth at certain words which, over time, have changed meanings, have become associated with different sets of values. Here—I'm going to write notes on the board while I talk, so listen now and copy afterwards. The author Raymond Williams says that 'correct' English keeps changing, and two of the words he examines are *community* and *individual.* For instance, on individuality he quotes the poet John Donne, back in the 1600s, *attacking* individuality in its then new meaning of 'idiosyncratic—a vain or eccentric departure from the common ground of human nature.' Donne complains that 'every man alone thinks he hath got / To be a Phoenix, and that then can be / None of that kind of which he is but he.' Phoenix? It's a mythological bird that after living five hundred years sets itself on fire, burns itself to death, and rises from its own ashes. Donne's not attacking individuality as egotism, the way you were—but as something irrational, abnormal, too quirky.

"Originally the word had meant 'something that can't be divided,' whereas today we tend to think of it as just the opposite—of an individual as someone who divides himself from the norm, from the group. Western thought didn't always celebrate individuality as a personal quality that was good to have. It wasn't even a personal quality at all. But gradually medieval feudalism broke down, and man was no longer just an insignificant part of a rigid hierarchy. Renaissance humanism is all about the significance of man, apart from his relationship to an overlord. And Protestantism developed around the same time, with its emphasis on each person having his own *individual* relation to God. Seventeenth-century math and logic 'postulated the individual as the substantial entity from which other categories were derived.' I'm still drawing from Williams here. With the Enlightenment came new theories of government—ideas about the rights of man—that helped pave the way for the concept of individuality as a significant quality. The idea of the social contract—you know about that from European History?— paid attention to the needs and rights of the individual—some of which society, or the state, had to meet in order to be legitimate. The French and American revolutions—late 1700s—celebrated the need for individual freedom, and around the same time, the Romantic movement in the arts— Blake, Wordsworth, Coleridge—extolled the uniqueness of each person's relation to nature—and the concept of original genius.[9]

"So," I conclude, "words aren't set in stone. Ralph Waldo Emerson wrote his famous essay called 'Self-Reliance' back in the mid-1800s. Does the title make you think of self-help books? Do you think people today feel any more dependent on 'experts' than people a hundred years ago? When do you suppose the phrase 'self-help' came into the language?"

"Like, 1980s," someone guesses.

We look it up: "*self-help* . . . [1825–35.]"

"I wonder what the first recorded use of it was? Words enter a language because there's some need for them. . . . Where could we go to find out?"

"Oh, that humungous dictionary in the library that has the magnifying glass!"

"Otherwise known as the *OED—Oxford English Dictionary*. Williams points out that even the august editors of the *OED* can't be certain about the first time a word's new meaning appeared in print. But the quotations and dates they give are really fascinating. Who's got a free period and could go look it up for tomorrow?" Silence. "Okay, I guess I'm the one who wants to know. I'll check it out." There are times when the larger speech community rules.

"Let's take our last twenty minutes and try writing our own dictionary definitions of *self* and *community*. [Thank goodness this is the seventy-minute period we get every two weeks!] You've been saying some really interesting things, exploring the vibes, the associations, these words have for you—which are certainly part of their meaning. But now see how you would 'standardize' your definitions—you know, find a kind of common denominator meaning that would work across the board—and write them down the way you think a dictionary would. You're allowed two or three definitions for each word, if you think they're necessary to cover all the bases, but don't bother about *self* as the reflexive pronoun—yourself, herself, etc.—and skip what they call 'the combining form'—as in *self-image* and all those other selfs. Come on, let's give it a try. You know what dictionaries sound like."

There are groans. With which I sympathize as I try doing it myself. Hesitating, I write: "Self . . . n. 1. the single, whole person; 2. the collection of traits that make up the personal identity. Community . . . n. 1. group of people who have things in common: the theater community. 2. group of individuals living together, mutually dependent, or the place where they live."

Some volunteers write their definitions on the board. They aren't much different from mine, though some of the *self* definitions offer synonyms such as *personality, psyche, ego,* and some of the *community* meanings include commune, town or city, neighborhood. One strong-minded lexicographer insists that *community* should include "requiring dangerous sacrifice of individuality for the good of the whole." I am reminded of some of Samuel Johnson's more opinionated definitions. And another student, defining *self,* writes "unchanging, nonconforming."

"Now let's look at the dictionary," somebody suggests. So we do, starting with Matt's little paperback *Random House Webster's.*

> **self** . . . **1.** a person or thing referred to with respect to complete individuality. **2.** a person's nature or character. **3.** personal interest.

> **community** . . . **1. a.** a group of people who reside in a specific locality and share government. **b.** such a locality. **2.** a group sharing common interests: the business community. **3.** joint possession or ownership. **4.** similar character; agreement: community of interests.

Then we turn to the classroom hardcover *Random House Webster's* and find some additional definitions:

> **self** . . . **4.** *Philos.* the subject of experience as contrasted with the object of experience; ego. **5.** any of the natural constituents of the body that are normally not subject to attack by components of the immune system.

And the derivations: before 900; Old English *self, selfa,* with connections to Old Norse, Old High German, Gothic, etc.

"Try using that fourth definition in relation to the different kinds of defining we've been doing," I suggest. "It refers to *subjectivity* and *objectivity.* Which word would you apply to the definitions you wrote down when you were trying to imitate the dictionary's approach to words? . . . Yes, 'objective.' You were trying to stand outside your own personal feelings and treat those words as objects. And which would you apply to whatever associations you brought up in discussion. . . . Okay, right, 'subjective.' And both approaches are important, to philosophers and to users of language, though each of you may be more comfortable, temperamentally, with one than the other."

For *community* we find that in addition to sharing government, members might share a cultural and historical heritage, and they might be a social, religious, or occupational group. Also the word could refer to: "**4.** the public; society," or "**5.** a group of associated nations sharing common interests or heritage," or "**6.** an assemblage of interacting plant and animal populations occupying a given area." Derivation was from 1325–1375; *comunete*, Middle French, and that went back to the Latin *communis* for *common*. We also find, to one student's delight, "**community service** . . . a punitive sentence requiring a convicted person to perform unpaid work for the community in lieu of imprisonment [1975–80]."

"Interesting that most of us didn't think of community as applying to any species other than our own," Mara comments.

Time is running out. I have been on the verge of bringing up *community values,* which neither dictionary has listed. But we need to move into our first reading assignment. I don't want to lose this initial focus on two words that are going to be at the heart of all our readings, as well as the basis for our work together as a group of individuals.

So I hand out an assignment sheet: "Today's Monday. For Wednesday, let's spend at least an hour and a half making something that explores your public self versus your private self—it could be masks, a poem, a scene to act out, a 'song of yourself.' . . . For instance, some people in this class know you much better than others do.  What are some of the different 'selves'— the different versions of 'you'—that might exist in the minds of various members of this group? What aspects of 'you' do your parents see? Is your grandmother's 'you' different from your dad's? Does your best friend see a different 'you' than your younger sister does? How about your dog? And who's the 'you' that you yourself know? Is it much different from the 'you' that you'd like to be? Which is the 'truer' you? Is it possible to be objective about this?

"Any questions? Be prepared to share what you've made in some way—I think we'll work in small groups, since it's early in the year and we won't have the whole period. We're also going to start Walt Whitman tomorrow, aloud—'Song of Myself.'"

## Notes

1. Peggy Rosenthal, *Words and Values* (New York: Oxford University Press, 1984). This book explores the ways in which loaded words such as *relationship, self, development, individual, potential, whole, consensus, relative,* and *community* control our public and private lives and how they acquired the hidden values and implications they carry. Drawing on history, semantics, and sociology, Rosenthal shows us how language that seems to be positive and liberating can entrap us without our knowledge.

2. Raymond Williams, *Keywords: A Vocabulary of Culture and Society,* rev. ed. (New York: Oxford University Press, 1985). Williams, a British cultural and social historian, originally designed this book as an appendix to his classic *Culture and Society, 1780–1950,* but gradually he expanded it to include 155 words and published it in book form in 1976. As words and society constantly evolve, however, he soon began adding new words and rewriting many of the original essays; his additional words include *ecology, generation,* and *sex.* The essays are fascinating reflections of society's changing values. The entry on *sex,* for example, begins by pointing out that while today the word is most commonly used to refer to physical relations between the sexes, in its early uses it was a description of the divisions between them.

3. Peter Elbow, *Writing without Teachers* (New York: Oxford University Press, 1998), 152–53. This is a book that, despite what the title might seem to imply, empowers teachers, for it invites us to think more broadly and deeply about the nature of learning and language. In particular, it considers the respective advantages of two different approaches to learning: faith and doubt. Elbow unites the powers of poet and philosopher, teacher and learner, realist and idealist.

4. Elbow, *Writing without Teachers,* 153.

5. Abram, *Spell of the Sensuous,* 99–100 (see note 8, chap. 3).

6. Elbow, *Writing without Teachers,* 151–52.

7. Elbow, *Writing without Teachers,* 154–56.

8. Elbow, *Writing without Teachers,* 167–68.

9. Williams, *Keywords,* 161–65.

# Chapter 5

# *Jump!*

## *Teachers' Convention*

*There is a moon, and a cow, there is a candle melting
white in a stick, I am jumping thirty-two times in
fluorescent lights amid white-clothed hotel
tables, jumping in a long, blue-flowered dress that I
bought loose to conceal what may be perfectly harmless
cysts, I am jumping to show these teachers how
their kids might jump into calm and poems and remembrance.
I jump out of my moon-eyed, owl-call fear of
incision, of losing babies I never had, I jump out of my mother's
skin and her quick-start cancer, jump through the moonstone
ring she left me, I jump with pointed toes, first, and discreet
legs, then come down hard, straight into the floor,
dogmatic and angular,* there are many ways
to kneel and kiss the ground. *Jump, I tell the anxious
teachers, shake the invisible, make the absent chandeliers
tremble and shed their leaves, they are the old
mischief, we must shake them down, jump!*[1]

*R*evisiting this poem, which I wrote two autumns ago just before I began six months of chemotherapy for cancer, feels strange—but also exhilarating. I was at the NCTE Annual Convention to give a presentation along with my best poet friend, who taught there in Detroit, and since I was due for exploratory surgery the following week, this weekend hundreds of miles away from home with a friend I rarely got to see felt like pure escape—the mouse's final leap before a hot-breathing cat caught up with it. But the jumping exercise I was doing with a group of unfamiliar women was one I did quite often with my students. I was taking off into the wild blue yonder but from a well-known springboard.

When it's the last period on a Friday, ninth graders do not want to stay in their seats, let alone discuss anything as abstract as language. The obligations of Monday are far off. These kids have already jumped into the weekend, into fantasy, into another kind of time and space. So we might as well try to make use of this particular kind of energy.

Erik Erikson writes well about leaping—both the physical and the imaginative kinds: "To truly leap, you must learn how to use the ground as a springboard, and how to land resiliently and safely. It means to test the leeway allowed by given limits; to outdo and yet not escape gravity; . . . to leap into make believe and yet be able to return to factual reality."[2]

I'm suddenly remembering a collection of photographs of various famous individuals jumping. There were demure jumps, frantic jumps, exuberant jumps, anxious jumps. All the jumpers were adults. Young children are the best jumpers, especially in public; they don't seem worried about how they look or why they are jumping. Ninth graders need more encouragement—even the basketball players. They want desperately to pass for "normal." They aren't yet as nostalgic for childhood spontaneity as twelfth graders are, or at least they aren't as ready to admit it, and they're less willing to trust that a teacher's craziness might lead them some place they'd like to go. They remember the lid that was kept on them in junior high school—the little leeway they had for all their energy and what happened when they tested the limits; they may not yet have experienced much independence as learners. And if the "vocabulary" they encountered came in workbooks rather than in the context of speech and writing, they probably don't feel very possessive about the words they have learned.

If we can free them up a little, physically—disorient them—they'll be readier to take language into their bodies, or even to find it there and instinctively translate it into words. This is also a means of discovering the good actors, dancers, the instinctive movers and clowns in the class and giving them some recognition. It signals that spontaneity and inventiveness will be valued in the classroom. Students with these particular gifts, sometimes very restless individuals who communicate best with their bodies, may well not have won much favor with their teachers and may already be viewing school as a lost cause. Introducing movement into a course that is basically about the written and spoken word makes an important connection for them—for everyone: that movement is a language and that speech is, in part, gesture. In writing about "the flesh of language," David Abram says, "We . . . learn our native language not mentally but bodily." And in referring to the philosopher Merleau-Ponty's *Phenomenology of Perception,* Abram notes, "he wrote at length of the gestural genesis of language, the way that communicative meaning is first incarnate in the gestures by which the body spontaneously expresses feelings and responds to changes in its affective environment."[3] It's important to help students recognize that studying "English" can involve a variety of languages—or, as Howard Gardner says, "intelligences"—and that some of us learn about words and express ourselves better by moving than by speaking or writing.

When I studied dance appreciation one summer at Lincoln Center, the teacher warmed us up and focused us with the following exercise: Eight jumps with the feet together; eight with feet turned out (heels touching, like first position in ballet); eight with feet apart and parallel; eight with legs apart and feet turned out—this last type nice and heavy, feeling yourself going down into the floor. Then four of each. Then two of each. Then—the hardest to coordinate—*one* of each. All sets at the same pace and rhythm. He counted: 1234567, turnout! 1234567, apart! 1234567, turnout! 1234567, again: 123turnout! 123apart!, etc. He also beat a drum—which I usually dispense with so that I can jump along with my students.

This Friday my ninth graders and I jump. We turn out the lights, which always seems to help prepare us to try the unfamiliar. I explain that this is not the same as jumping jacks in the gym—that they'll have to listen and probably watch me the first time through. Everyone likes the last set of eight once they've gotten over the need to be graceful and can let themselves thump hard into the floor "like a Mack truck." We have to repeat the final set of one each again and again till everyone gets it. By this time, we're all panting and laughing. We've reached that kind of focus—relaxed but concentrating—that seems to work best for learning and creating. So I can risk a question that, had we all been sitting at desks, might feel abstract, boring, or too difficult, too gigantic: "How do you suppose talking ever got started? I mean, where might the first words on earth have come from?"

We flop to the floor. Circle up.

"How about from the animals," Courtney says. "Growls and roars and hisses and stuff like that. Maybe to let another hunter know what kind of animal they just killed."

"Maybe cavewoman got bored while caveman was out hunting, and she started to draw pictures on the wall. And then she made up sounds to explain the pictures."

"Maybe the first word was *Ouch*. Like for the first toothache in the world. Or the first time a guy stubbed his toe."

"I bet it was when they started kissing, and it felt good so they went, 'Mmmm.'"

"Maybe they started humming or beating with a rock and got the idea for other kinds of sounds."

"How about they imitated the rain or the waves or the wind?"

"Hey, wait a minute, you know those Africans who make a click when they talk, I forget what they're called, but maybe people started making sounds with their teeth or clapped their hands—or maybe it started with dancing. Or their stomachs rumbling."

This last idea makes me think of some lines in a poem I like by Naomi Shihab Nye: "My toes are dictionaries. / Do you need any words?" [4]

"These are all neat ideas, and since I don't think any experts have an answer, let's play around with this last one a little. Let's list parts of our bodies and then list different things they do—maybe not just noises they make, like stomach rumbles, but action, like skin itching. I'll bet our bodies are full of verbs. Here, I know. Think about all the names of body parts—include some of the fancy words you know from biology—and we'll get them up on the board. Then we'll split into groups for the lower, middle, and upper body and see what verbs we can get."

We list: toes, heels, feet, ankles, metatarsals, shins, knees, legs, thighs, hips, stomach, abdomen, pancreas, kidneys, intestines, arms, elbows, etc. And we end up with plenty of sounds—tiptoe, tap, stamp, stomp, kick, rumble, growl, tap, drum, punch, crack, creak, snore, rattle, yawn, lick, grind, sniffle, flap, rustle, click, slap, smack, kiss, chew, chomp, cough, spit, slurp, choke. And plenty of action: flex, sprain, tread, slip, slide, curl, dig, kneel, jerk, swivel, swing, undulate, bend, twist, bloat, shrink, embrace, hug, cling, swing, sock, throw, hurl, toss, caress, stroke, pet, knead, juggle, wave, press, clench, splay, shake, fold, interlace, flick, scrape, crook, shrug, jut, point, pinch, roll, crane, stretch, ache, pivot, wag, nod, stream, curl, bristle, shake, blink, twitch, wink, pierce, lift, lower, beetle, grimace, frown, smile, wince, foam, water, purse, pout, chew, salivate, clench, run, listen, prick up, wiggle, flap.

So the body *is* a dictionary. When we read these verbs on the page, we can experience their kinesthetic equivalent. And when we use them in writing, we're enabling the reader to have the same sensations—to be, for a moment, more fully alive. To encounter the living, leaping word.

In order to help students appreciate more fully the various qualities of movement and, as writers, choose their verbs more precisely, I like to introduce them to the Laban energies. Rudolf Laban observed these movement qualities when, in the 1920s, he was asked to study the efficiency of factory workers' movements. He broke down his observations into eight energies—*flick, slash, tap, punch, press, wring, glide, float.* These categories were later used in notating dance moves, and theater directors also use them sometimes to help actors discover their character's particular physicality in a given speech or scene. Each of the qualities can be classified as fast or slow, direct or indirect, and light or heavy. I lead the class in trying out some of these energies, first with our hands, then with arms, feet, heads, and hips, and finally in traveling across the floor. We wring our hands, we wring out an invisible dripping towel, we wring our legs together.

"I'm getting a headache," Ted complains.

"*Wring* is real heavy," Jen offers, "and slow."

We try to wring our way around the room, but it's hard to cover any territory this way.

"I'm getting nowhere fast," Ted grunts.

"Direct or indirect?" I ask him.

"It's like something eating away at you inside, like a guilty conscience," somebody says. "It's what Iago does to Othello."

"Let's add to our list of verbs," I say. "Try moving through mud. What verb best captures this? Watch what it looks like on other people, as well as how it feels in your own body. . . . Now through jello . . . now through a jungle full of tigers. . . . Move like it's just before the end of the game on the basketball court. . . . Now on horseback . . . now through wet leaves . . . now on a sultry afternoon in the Tropics. . . . Now climb a tree."

I ask them to consider how they move when they're feeling scared, how they move when they're feeling suspicious, and how to differentiate between these two energies. What about unsure versus nervous? How about moving like a cat versus moving like a lion? Like a volcano versus like glue? A squirrel versus a minnow?

We add to our verb lists, and I collect them. Then I break the class into groups and hand each group a few of the most promising-looking lists. "Choose three verbs to act out for the rest of us to guess," I tell them. "You may perform as a group, or in pairs, or in solo, but confer and try out moves together before you decide. Consider what kind of energy and movement your word is: speed, weight, directness, low or medium or high." And I send them to separate corners of the room.

When we're ready to perform, I remind everyone to watch for these categories as they try to guess. When a verb is guessed correctly, we all add it to our individual lists, along with a definition based on the movement qualities: *skitter*—move quickly, lightly, side to side over the top of a surface. I might ask what kind of creature moves this way, so we can add an example to the definition—"like a dragonfly," "like a water bug." When a movement seems to fit several different words, I ask whether these verbs—*dart* and *skitter*—might in fact be synonyms, and if so, is there still a little difference, a matter of connotation, maybe, or is the difference simply in the sound of the word? Is *scuttle* a little more negative, less innocent and happy, than *scamper*? Which creatures scuttle and which creatures scamper? Roaches versus kittens? How about human beings—might a child scamper across the grass to elude the babysitter, while a throng of frightened civilians scuttles down into a bomb shelter? What impression does *scuttle* give us of these civilians?

So much depends on context. This is a lesson in analyzing and appreciating literary style—a lesson for both the reader and the writer. But it can be learned through the body: how does *scamper* feel different from *scuttle* when you do them both, or when your senses register someone else doing them? It's important that we not lose the physicality of language that was so vividly and instinctively a part of us when we were children.

Of course, looking up the derivations of these verbs can also help us lodge their meanings in our senses. *Slog*—to hit hard as in boxing, or to plod heavily—is listed as "akin to *slug*," which comes from Swedish and Norwegian *sluggje*—a heavy, slow person. *Undulate*, used by seventeenth-century physicists to describe the motion of a wave, comes from the Latin *undulatus*, "wavy," and, logically enough, can also refer to a sound that rises and falls in pitch. *Shimmy* was the name of a 1920s ragtime dance marked by rapid shaking of hips and shoulders and is also used to describe extreme wobbling in the front wheels of a car, but originally it derived from the nickname for *chemise—shimmy*, a woman's loose undergarment or shift.

This is a good time to read—and act out—Lewis Carroll's poem "Jabberwocky." Although most of Carroll's verbs can be found in the dictionary, and some have been around for hundreds of years, students may not know this and will rely mainly on sound, rather than denotation: how does one gimbol in the wabe? Whiffle? Burble? Galumph? These words usually inspire them to make up some of their own. Some kids will try a move and then find a name for it; others will start with a sound. Remind them to let sound and action interact. To clunge seems to call for some combination of cling and lunge—perhaps lunging into an embrace? Ask them to provide some irregular forms: to clunge, clang, clungen? Might clunge be a noun as well as a verb? Demonstrate a clunge.

For the weekend, I ask them to make a list of nouns to try using with some of their verbs, but because I want to move them into metaphor, I ask them to avoid listing types of *people.* Instead I pass out a sheet with specific categories: buildings, weather, time units, animals/birds/fish/plants/stones, geological formations, heavenly bodies, and emotions. "Be imaginative," I urge. "Think about cultures and parts of the country that are different from yours, consider using foreign words, go for interesting sounds."

The sheet also directs them to write ten sentences, each one combining one of their nouns with one of their verbs. "Let yourself experiment; don't go for predictable combinations. When you've finished, circle one sentence you could imagine using as the start of a poem, one for the opening of a story, and one for somebody's diary entry. If you get inspired, write one of these three pieces. Have a good weekend!"

On Monday, our lists contain mistrals and typhoons, cumulus clouds and blizzards, malls and wombs, April Fool's Day and the end of summer, cascades and comets, asteroids and red dwarfs, panic and melancholy and anxiety attacks. Some of my favorite student sentences include:

Love winked at her from behind the door.
That was the morning his house kicked him out.
He tried to sleep, but midnight bristled around him.
She was so depressed she could hear the grass ache.
Summer was already undulating toward its end.

## Notes

1. Judith Michaels, "Teachers' Convention," *Nimrod: International Journal of Prose and Poetry*, 42.2 (Spring/Summer 1999): 71.

2. Eric Erikson, *Toys and Reasons: Stages in the Ritualization of Experience*, quoted by Jonathan Cott, *Pipers at the Gates of Dawn* (New York: Random House, 1983), 35. Subtitled *The Wisdom of Children's Literature*, this book consists of seven essay-interviews in which Cott reflects on the creative riches of childhood and children's literature along with his subjects: Dr. Seuss, Maurice Sendak, William Steig, Astrid Lindgren, Chinua Achebe, P. L. Travers, and Iona Opie and Peter Opie. The book reminds those of us mired in vocabulary lists and tests how rewarding it can be to play with language, to risk nonsense. It ends with a passage by Peter Opie, a notable scholar of children's lore, games, and language, written nine months before he died:

> I happen to believe that life is nonsense, that we're an accident, that there is no life after death, and that there is no reason for one being here other than being here. Now, good nonsense is wonderful because it frees the mind, it's like one's dreams, it makes you realize that nothing matters very much. And it seems to me that if you appreciate nonsense, then you're really getting wise. That's the great freedom, because you can then make up your own rules.

This is followed by some lines written by the Russian poet Osip Mandelstam from the concentration camp where he died:

> *Mounds of human heads are wandering into the distance.*
> *I dwindle among them. Nobody sees me. But in books*
> *much loved, and in children's games I shall rise*
> *from the dead to say the sun is shining.*

3. Abram, *The Spell of the Sensuous,* 74 (see note 8, chap. 3).

4. Naomi Shihab Nye, "One Boy Told Me," *Fuel: Poems* (Rochester, NY: BOA Editions, 1998), 31–33.

# Chapter 6

# True/False: Revisiting Holden Caulfield

I t would be hard to discuss *Antigone* without defining civil disobedience, even though that's not an expression Sophocles used. *Oedipus Rex* inevitably leads to a discussion of fate and freewill; *The Grapes of Wrath* to capitalism, socialism, and communism; *Macbeth* to ambition; *Hamlet* to ambivalence. And *The Catcher in the Rye* invites a consideration of the word *phony.*

*Phony* is a particularly fruitful word to explore with students. They themselves are quick to judge people as "fake" or "hypocritical," and they place a high value on sincerity, but their feelings about Holden Caulfield tend to be mixed. "He's always so negative. Isn't there anything he likes?" they ask impatiently—along with Holden's worried little sister Phoebe. "He's a hypocrite himself—he hates fake people, but he's always lying. He even says so." "He's worse than phony. At least all those people he thinks are so fake are able to get along with their lives. He can't cope with the real world at all. He's paranoid. He ends up in a mental clinic." For many of our students, ambivalence is not an option.

So we go back to the text to look more closely at Holden's world, to see if he's right about at least some of its phoniness, to consider what and whom he values as authentic and which of his catchphrases let us know this, and to talk about the phonies *we've* encountered—maybe even the times we've felt like phonies ourselves. Since the students enjoy imitating Holden's voice, and usually end up writing a piece in that voice, I want them to think about the ways in which a character's language conveys his attitudes toward himself and his world—both his conscious attitudes and those he's not fully aware of. They begin to notice, as they collect "Holden" words to use in their pieces, that he says "really" a lot (which I remind them comes from *real*)—that it's a kind of defense against the phoniness he sees everywhere and even against his own tendency to invent, fantasize, "lie." And they eventually recognize that the people and the moments he cherishes all possess a spontaneity, a genuineness, and an innocence that he associates with children. These are the qualities he sees imperiled by the grown-up world of phoniness and corruption—a world he'd like to escape. These are the qualities he clings to as "real." If he has to grow up, he doesn't want to become a lawyer like his father, who has to defend the phonies, but rather a protector of children.

When we look up *phony*, we find that some dictionaries list it as U.S. slang. It's not a word that my students use. So this is a good opportunity to explore the nature of slang—and jargon and argot. And to clarify the difference between these terms and colloquial language. *Argot*, which came into use in the 1850s from the French *argoter* (to quarrel), refers to "a specialized vocabulary . . . and idiom," sometimes "devised for private communication and identification," as in "*thieves' argot.*"[1] *Jargon* came down from the Old French *gargun*, which may have derived from an expressive base related to *gargle* and *gargoyle.* (Now whenever I find myself irritated by critical jargon, I can just dismiss it as gargling.) It had entered Middle English by the 1300s. Its more neutral meaning is simply language "peculiar to a particular trade, profession, or group," but it also can refer to "unintelligible talk or writing, . . . characterized by uncommon or pretentious vocabulary, . . . convoluted syntax, . . . and vague[ness] of meaning"; "gibberish, babble."[2] I think of a Dave Barry column I just read in which he's taking on the role of Mister Language Person and gives an example of how to correct jargon: "When writing a business report avoid big words and jargon; try to use everyday language. WRONG: 'We will prioritize the infrastructure paradigm matrices.' RIGHT: "We are fixin' to prioritize the infrastructure paradigm matrices.'"[3]

At this point, we pause while I ask the class to add the new words and synonyms to their notebooks—and to taste the imitative sounds of *gibberish* and *babble* compared to the dignity of the Latinate *pretentious* and *convoluted*. The Latin students take a stab at the prefixes and roots, and I point out how the verb *volvere*—to roll or twist—began as a physical action and got extended to a metaphorical description of style. I mention the flower convolvulus, the morning glories that twine around trellises. "Imagine a style of writing that carried this to an extreme, not gracefully but to the point of twisting up the meaning."

"Do you think *pretentious* is related in any way to phoniness? Are the people Holden labels as phony making a conscious *pretense* at something? Does one have to *work* at being a phony, or is it second nature? And do any of the people whose tastes strike Holden as pretentious—like Sally's love of the Lunts—merely have different tastes from his? Or does Salinger want us to identify with Holden's view? Let's look at some of the things Sally actually says. . . ."

The entry for *slang* says the derivation is uncertain and gives a date of 1750–1760. The primary definition is "very informal usage in vocabulary and idiom that is characteristically more metaphorical, playful, elliptical, vivid, and ephemeral than ordinary language." We discuss the meaning of these words. *Idiom* is hard for the students, but examples from foreign languages help, and it's a great opportunity to look at those usages students always confuse, such as *different from* versus *different than, among* versus *between, number* versus *amount, farther* versus *further, fewer* versus *less.* Then we go on to the additional meanings of *slang:* "speech or writing characterized by the use of vulgar and socially taboo vocabulary and idiomatic expressions."[4] They've already asked, enthusiastically, whether they're allowed to use Holden's "hell" and "damn" when they write in his voice, and I ask whether they really think of those expressions as taboo nowadays. We get into the current equivalents for Salinger's "flicks" (gays) and discuss which terms they consider objectionable.

"So teach me the slang I should know if I want to write in the voice of a modern fourteen-year-old," I beg my students. They make a brief list. "We don't use all that much," they insist. They're cool; they won't let me in on it. Or they're so used to it that they don't see it as slang.

"Suppose you were writing a short story with lots of dialogue among the teenage characters. What would you use? *Cheesy*—you call everything you don't like 'cheesy.' You've even got me doing it. What about any of these?" And I read from my slang dictionary's Teen/College section: "'*blade, bone out, box tonsils, eddie, Do you see skid marks on my forehead?, No wire hangers!*'—what in God's name does that last one mean?"

They giggle. And I read the definition: "'Please don't do this anymore!; from a well-known scene in the film *Mommie Dearest*.'"[5] Well, it's *vivid* and *metaphorical*, I guess. And as far as I'm concerned, *elliptical*.

"So what are the pluses and minuses of slang? It's vivid language. It makes you feel part of an in-group. It's fun to use. It makes it easier to talk about taboo things—like what?"

"Oh, sex," Sam says, with a world-weary sigh. "And drinking and drugs."

"Yeah, and disgusting things like puking and snot," Jon adds. "It's kind of like using—what's that word that makes bad stuff sound okay—like 'passing away' instead of 'dying'?"

"*Euphemisms.* Well, but sometimes the slang for taboo things sounds worse than the more formal word. Dysphemisms. You have some words for vomit that sound *much* worse."

"It's also a good way to put down people who you resent, who are obnoxious, who get in your way," Sam says happily.

"Well, but sometimes it lets you get away with being racist or sexist," Pat objects. "You say these things in your little group and it sounds funny. But if an outsider heard you, they'd think you were pretty disgusting."

"Yes," I agreed. "There are a lot of put-down words for women in this slang dictionary—just women in general, not even obnoxious women. Whereas the put-downs for men seem to be for a few specific types—computer 'nerds,' mostly. The introduction to the book does make a point of saying that it's left out terms that refer to sexual preference or ethnic background, but it says nothing about gender. Its purpose is to provide a collection of 'practical, useful terms employed every day in business and popular language.'[6]

"It characterizes two sorts of slang—'mysterious, private lingoes of microcosms such as teenagers, criminals, lawyers, doctors'—I love those juxtapositions—and then the 'widely used and longstanding idiomatic phrases that continue to be the backbone of the spoken shorthand that is slang.' I like that word *shorthand*. I think Holden's use of *phony* is complicated because it *is* shorthand for him. It stands for all sorts of views and behavior he finds objectionable. The intro to this dictionary also has a warning against using slang if you're not absolutely certain about its meaning or what contexts to use it in. Have you learned any slang in your foreign language courses? Do you read foreign newspapers or cartoons? Remember the Monty Python routine with the Hungarian who has an English phrase book that misleads him into making lewd invitations?

"Of course, once slang makes it into the dictionary, it's not cool anymore, is it? It's on its way to becoming public, mainstream. This recent Random House dictionary (1997) lists *phony* but doesn't even call it slang, whereas this old dictionary from the forties does have 'sl' next to it. It's really interesting to look at the lists in the front of this *Random House Webster's* of words that came into the dictionary during specific decades in this half of the century—not necessarily slang, but words that we needed in order to talk and think about new inventions and developments or new ways of looking at things. You get a feel for U.S. history in a way that you don't get from your history textbooks." And I hand out lists. The 1940s reflect, of course, the war, with A-bomb, ack-ack, airlift, bazooka, bloodmobile, buzz bomb, displaced person, genocide, G-suit, jet plane, missile, Molotov cocktail, plutonium, quisling, radar. But also food and fashion—bikini, bobbysoxer, carhop, cheeseburger, falsie, freeze-dry, pedal pushers—and entertainment—bebop, hot rod, long-playing, party pooper, quiz show, show biz, snorkel, tape recorder.

"Remember, this is the decade that Holden was living in—records, not CDs (remember the record he buys for Phoebe?), and jazz clubs rather than rock concerts. Do you think there was a teen culture back then in the same sense there is now? What kind of movies does Holden talk about—remember, when he's been punched out by the pimp and he imagines himself in a movie? What drinks does he order? Any fast food or junk food? Who are his idols? Does he mention any TV shows? The lists of words decade by decade trace the developments in all sorts of areas—politics, sports, the arts, psychology, food, family life, business, race, medicine, technology."

We browse the lists. Then I give them an assignment: Look up *phony*—find its meanings, derivations, and as many synonyms or related words as possible. Include nouns, verbs, and adjectives, since *phony* can be all of these. Think about what's "phony" in specific categories—in money, the arts, advertising, food, clothing, relationships, nature. And think about the antonyms of *phony—real, true.* What are some of the things we most want, or expect, to be true or real? Think about both concrete things and abstractions. You can use a thesaurus. You can talk to older siblings and adults; think about people who might have expertise in special areas. What shades of difference can you find between synonyms—for instance, a *phony* versus a *hypocrite*? Would you use these two in exactly the same way? In the same situation? In the same kinds of writing?

Next day the students come in with their findings. They've discovered the Phony War. They know that *phony* may have come from *fawney,* a finger ring (Irish *fsptainne*) used in a fawney rig—street argot for a confidence game in which a brass ring is sold as a gold one. Around 1895 *phony up* was being used as a verb—to fake, to phony up a document. Some of the kids had assumed the word has the same root as all the *phone* words, though they couldn't figure out what it would have to do with "sound" or "voice." Still, they had happily listed as related words *telephone, saxophone, phonetic, phonograph,* etc. The rest of us disabuse them.

Dictionaries had offered them some synonyms for a variety of contexts: *fake, not real or genuine,* as in phony diamonds; *false* or *deceiving,* as in a phony excuse; *affected* (a word most of them didn't know) or *pretentious,* or an *insincere* person; a *counterfeit;* (verb) *to falsify.*

"So the word can be used to describe an action or a thing—both a concrete and an abstract thing, a diamond or an excuse—or a person," I summarize. "It sounds like it can refer to deliberate deception but also to a sort of unconscious way of behaving that you might get so accustomed to, you wouldn't even realize this wasn't your genuine self. Or maybe it's become who you really are.

"Let's get some of your related words up on the board and see what categories they fall into." Students volunteer *crocodile tears, to bluff, to gloss over, plastic*—(I think of Dustin Hoffman in *The Graduate,* being told by his dad's friend that the secret of life is "plastics," and I also think of overextended credit cards)—*disguise, alias, hypocrite, camouflage, scam, hype, makeover, fake-bake* (tan from a salon), *suck up, kiss up, apple polish, flatter, sycophant, impostor, evasive, defraud, mislead, feign, sham, plagiarist, cheat, fraudulent, con artist, false front, artificial, unnatural, synthetic, polyester, aspartame, trick, fabricate, cosmeticize, ostentatious, underhanded.*

I add *trompe l'oeil, facade, falsies, spurious, bogus, inauthentic, fawn on, equivocate, prevaricate, obsequious,* and—one of my favorites—*ersatz.*

"So what kind of voice, what kind of character, might you create if you made her or him use words like *prevaricate, fraudulent, sycophant, pretentious, obsequious, fabricate, ostentatious, falsify?*" I ask them. "Get a picture in your mind—age, style of dress and hair, stance, gesture, situation—who's the person speaking to? Is this narration, or dialogue? And what about someone who's using *con, fake, bluff, scam?*

"And which of our words are the most fun to say aloud?" The votes go to *bogus, scam, ersatz, suck up, sycophant, sham,* and *falsies*.

I assign the students to look up the words that no one can quite define, so that by the next day we'll have a complete list of definitions for our notebook collections and can try applying some of them to specific moments in *Catcher in the Rye*.

"What about the antonyms of *phony*?" I ask—and students list *sincere, truthful, verified, accurate, genuine, real, honest, legitimate, trustworthy, honorable, authentic, natural, pure. . . .*

I hand out a sheet to complicate things further: "Polonius, a character you'll meet next year in *Hamlet*, says to his son, 'This above all, to thine own self be true, and it must follow as the night the day, thou can'st not then be false to any man.' Do you think that's true? And are there different kinds of truth? Can two apparently contradictory things both be true? Could both your mother's view of your boyfriend and your own view of him be true? Are some truths truer than others? Or is truth absolute? What's the kind of truth that we think of as 'straight from the heart?' Do you always come across as genuine to other people when you speak straight from the heart? What's the kind of truth embodied in a law of physics or one of Euclid's theorems? Is the tree the botanist studies truer than the tree the poet sees that becomes a symbol by the end of her poem? What about the tree I remember from my first front yard?"

And on the board I write the terms *literal, figurative, empirical, ideal, representation, abstract art, symbolic, paradoxical, subjective, objective*.

"Which of these terms are you a bit hazy about?" I ask them. We deal with *empirical* and, very briefly, with *ideal* and Plato's theory of ideas—which some of them remember from Ancient Civ. class. "Now let's freewrite on the word *true* for the last fifteen minutes. We can spend some more time tonight on it, but let's get started now. You can start with the quote from Polonius, or from any of the kinds of 'truths' on the board. You can start with a free association for five minutes—just let the pencil keep writing, starting with the word *true*. You could start with true/false tests and what you think about them. Or the phrase 'true-to-life.' Anywhere."

Tomorrow, after I figure out some efficient means by which everyone can share their findings, I think we'll pair up to write dialogue journals back and forth on "the truth about Holden."

# Notes

1. *Random House Webster's College Dictionary,* 71 (see note 4, chap. 3).

2. *Random House Webster's College Dictionary,* 701 (see note 4, chap. 3).

3. Dave Barry, "How Speaking Efficiently Can Improve Your Sex Life," *The Conway Daily Sun* (25 June 1999).

4. *Random House Webster's College Dictionary,* 1213 (see note 4, chap. 3).

5. *21st Century Dictionary of Slang,* 328–34 (see note 2, chap. 3).

6. *21st Century Dictionary of Slang,* v (see note 2, chap. 3).

# "wholly to be a fool"

since feeling is first
who pays any attention
to the syntax of things
will never wholly kiss you;

wholly to be a fool
while Spring is in the world
my blood approves,
and kisses are a better fate
than wisdom
lady i swear by all flowers. Don't cry
—the best gesture of my brain is less than
your eyelids' flutter which says

we are for each other: then
laugh, leaning back in my arms
for life's not a paragraph

And death i think is no parenthesis

E. E. Cummings[1]

*M*ost students would go along with this sentiment, even though they don't have a clue what "syntax" is. Substitute "grammar," and they'd agree even more wholeheartedly.

There are holy fools and wholly fools, jesters and clowns and buffoons and class cutups. What they all have in common is a disregard for convention, whether social or linguistic. Dostoyevsky's holy fools are sublimely innocent of the norm and possess an intuitive ability to see beyond it, to connect with their world in embarrassingly empathic ways. Shakespeare's fools possess the wit to see through the accepted hierarchies of court life and the conventional meanings of words; they are dazzling jugglers of pun and paradox. Intuition, empathy, wit, and disregard for convention are also marks of the great writer. In helping students tune their ears—and mouths and eyes, even their fingertips, their nerve endings—to the glorious range of ways they can string words together, we need to encourage them to fool around, to experiment, to break rules even before they know all the rules.

Who ever knows *all* the rules, anyway?

And how absurd they can be. Having struggled to teach myself enough German to pass the foreign language requirements for my graduate work, I cherish Mark Twain's observation: "In German, a young lady has no sex, but a turnip has."[2]

In *The Story of English*, the companion book to the PBS television series of a decade ago, our language is admitted to be "maddeningly inconsistent in spelling and pronunciation," but praised for having a grammar "of great simplicity and flexibility. . . . Nouns can become verbs and verbs nouns in a way that is impossible in other languages. We can *dog* someone's footsteps. We can *foot it* to the bus. We can *bus* children to school and then *school* them in English." The authors speculate that the reason our language developed into so supple a one that its "arts of speech and literature have been perhaps the special contribution of the English people to European culture" may have something to do with its history:

> After the Norman invasion, English was neglected and ill-considered by the Latin-writing and French-speaking authorities; so it was unregulated and unimposed upon; from the earliest times it was naturally the language of protest and dissent, the language of the many rather than the few. Its genius was, and still is, essentially democratic. It has given expression to the voice of freedom from

Wat Tyler, to Tom Paine, to Thomas Jefferson, to Edmund Burke, to the Chartists, to Abraham Lincoln, to the Suffragettes, to Winston Churchill, to Martin Luther King.[3]

Too often, young students of English graduate with the conviction that it's all about rules. So it's a good idea to let them see how Shakespeare—and Lincoln and Twain and Cummings and Hemingway and Alice Walker and James Joyce and Sandra Cisneros and Samuel Beckett and Sherman Alexie —have taken advantage of the language's suppleness and broken any number of rules. In fact, the authors of *The Story of English* suggest that today,

in its new global state, English is probably finding more variety of expression and more local colour than at any time since the Elizabethan "golden age." When the language was confined to English and North American shores, it became progressively schooled by generations of grammars and dictionaries. Although that tradition lives on, its influence is counterbalanced by the sheer teeming diversity of the language in the age of mass communications, from the "Spanglish" of Miami and Los Angeles, to the "Slanguage" of the Antipodes, even the jargon of astronauts and computer hackers. Beyond the Anglo-American hegemony, there are newer English-using cultures for whom the precepts of Dr. Johnson and Noah Webster are not binding. The Indianization and Africanization of English is introducing a multi-cultural dimension to the language that is without precedent in the history of any language. . . . From this international perspective, the kaleidoscope of English today is perhaps closer in spirit and self-expression to the Shakespearian extravaganza than at any time since the seventeenth century. Spoken and written, it offers a medium of almost limitless potential and surprise.[4]

When my ninth graders asked whether they could actually use "hell" and "damn" when writing in Holden Caulfield's voice, they sounded surprised to hear me say, "Sure." Their writing, in these first few weeks of school, had been worried, cautious, roundabout, uninspired, lacking even limited "potential and surprise." This fact troubled me much more than the misspellings, run-ons, fragments, and repetitions—all of which, had they served an artistic purpose "arising," as Whitman said, "out of needs, tears, joys, affections, tastes," could have worked just fine.[5]

As we played around with our daily word collections, I found myself thinking of ways to break down their caution and break open the conventions of usage and syntax. I was fairly sure that permission to experiment would sooner or later develop in these kids a greater interest in the conventions themselves. One morning I read to them a piece of doggerel composed for foreign students struggling with English:

> *Beware of* heard, *a dreadful word*
> *That looks like* beard *and sounds like* bird,
> *And* dead: *It's said like* bed, *not* bead—
> *For goodness' sake, don't call it* deed![6]

I followed it up by handing out the introduction Richard Lederer wrote to a long and ingenious homophonic poem and inviting them to read it aloud:

> Hears a rye peace eye maid up inn my idol thyme. Aye Rote it four yew two sea Howe homophones Cannes seam sew whiled from there knows down too they're tows. With pried, eye no it will knot boar ewe. Its meant two bee red allowed.[7]

"But it's full of mistakes," Jen objected at first glance. "I'm always mixing up too and two like that."

"I like this guy," Mark said.

"Let's play around with some of this foolishness," I suggested. "I'll say a few sounds, and you write down as many words and spellings you can think of that fit the sound. Keep repeating the sound to yourself. Try using it in different parts of an imaginary sentence; if the first word you come up with is a person, place, or thing, try it out as an action or description, too. Start with *do*—the first note of the do re mi scale."

And they gave me *dough, doe, do, dew, due, dodo,* and *doo-doo* (as in what former President Bush said he was deep in). "Okay, and now *sol*, the fifth note in the scale." Pretty soon one of the girls was humming, "Do, a deer, a female deer, re, a drop of golden sun"—not one of my favorite songs, but I'd known what I was letting myself in for. We got *sole* the fish, *sole* of the shoe, *sole* as in only or alone or one, and *soul*.

"And then there's Sol—a name for the sun," I added, "related to *solstice*, and, while we're at it, what other sol/sun words can you think of for your notebook?" They came up with *solar system, solar wind, solarium, solar eclipse, solar home, solar year*.

"And what about *solar plexus*—how's that related to sun?" Jake asked.

"Haven't a clue," I said. "Here, I'll look it up and we'll find out." (I have learned from experience that too many "Why don't *you* look it up's" can lead to a rapid loss of curiosity.)

"Oh, it's from the 1700s—named because on that part of the stomach— you know, where you lose your breath and double up if you're punched there—the nerve patterns look like rays. So Jake, if you drew us a picture, you could make the rays *look* like how the punch would *feel*—like in a cartoon. That would be a way to remember. And to punch someone who hadn't punched you would be, at least in refined, civilized classrooms, a *solecism*. Anybody know what that means?"

"Something rude? Unfair? Something against the rules?" Jake guessed.

"Right—against the rules. 'Inappropriate,' as authorities are fond of saying whenever you really want to do something. It's also used more specifically to mean something that goes against standard rules of grammar. A lot of stuff that really interesting, original writers come up with are *solecisms* by conventional standards. And I have no idea where the word comes from. I bet it's not related to the sun." It wasn't, but the source was fascinating—a Latinism from the 1500s derived from the Greek *soloikismós,* from the city of Solo in Cilicia, where a corrupt form of Attic Greek was spoken. "See," I said, "there have always been William Safires—even way back then in Cilicia, and also when Shakespeare was spelling his name three different ways. For tonight, let's collect words that we can get a lot of mileage out of by spelling them various ways or using them different ways and with different meanings.

"Word play is great for poetry writing. Here, I'll show you, as an example of where this can lead, a sestina one of the juniors in my poetry class wrote, using the same six words over and over in different ways for the endings of the lines. One of the words he chose—or that chose him, because writing, especially poetry, works in funny ways sometimes—was *sole*. Sestinas are fun—if you let the sounds and the pictures of the six words lead you, in-stead of trying too hard to lead them. Trevor loves climbing mountains—I think he finds it a kind of spiritual thing—so in a way the choice of *sole/soul* was perfectly logical, but he said he was surprised at where his six words took him. Sestinas are traditionally written in six stanzas of six lines each (*sestina* comes from the Italian for 'six'), with a three-line closing. The six key words repeat at the ends of lines; the last word of the first stanza's final line becomes the last word of the next stanza's opening line," and I drew the scheme on the board:

| first stanza | second stanza |
|:---:|:---:|
| A | F |
| B | A |
| C | E |
| D | B |
| E | D |
| F | C |

"And so on, through the six stanzas. If you're really inspired, all six words get used in a final three-line stanza or 'envoy,' but not all modern sestinas do this. Ideally, the six key words should be ones you could use as different parts of speech, maybe with different meanings (maybe spelled in several different ways)—to give you as much flexibility, lead your imagination as fluidly, as possible. Suppose you chose the word *fire*. It could be a noun—both concrete, like a campfire or the brightness of something like a diamond, and abstract, like passion or enthusiasm. It could also be a verb— to dismiss from a job, or to inflame with emotion, or to shoot or throw, or to bake a clay pot in a kiln. Or it could be an adjective or part of a compound word—*firefly, fireplace, firelight, firecracker.* Here's Trevor's poem. Notice how in some stanzas he worked with long lines and in some with shorter ones; he really stretched the traditions of the form:"

### Mountain Bass

*On top of mountain*
*the ebb of Earth's bass*
*was keenly felt creeping through boots,*
*penetrating and bouncing captivated souls.*
*We stood, too tired to move, silence.*
*We sat down, fingers cut on rocks.*

*Metal bars were forever holding onto the rocks,*
*huge rock-metal steps to make it up the mountain,*
*footfall and panting broke the silence*

*as wind and hail hit us in our eyes like lead bass,*
*and our souls*
*were insulated by rubber-soled boots.*

*Slowly, upward we dragged our boots,*
*and when we slipped knees were skinned on rocks.*
*Souls*
*fitted us, trees, mountain,*
*I didn't miss car-radio bass,*
*instead my heart sang silence.*

*Furious trees and chipmunks wish to silence*
*our Malaysian manufactured boots.*
*The sun's bass*
*rocks*
*even the mountain;*
*weighted down with urban souls.*

*Ours are urban souls, monster truck souls, pimped out gremlin*
*souls,*
*and the quietest sound we know is air vent blowing, ear ringing*
*silence.*
*Ah, but mountain!*
*Mountain has known feet, has known socks, has known boots.*
*Slowly, thousands of us make the pilgrimage, wearing down the*
*rocks.*
*Traveling, heads bobbing to walkman-enhanced bass,*

*but I want to hear real bass.*
*Bass of souls,*
*Bass of rocks,*
*Bass of silence,*
*(ignoring my brown boots)*
*I hike mountain.*

*As 1,000,000 people climb I can hear the mountain bass,*
*but my false boots' souls*
*silence the red, red rocks.*

When Trevor wrote, later, about this poem, he said,

> I wondered, before writing the sestina, how a poem, a free-form
> thing, could ever come to me already in some predestined shape. I
> waited to find out. I waited and it found me. Lines came to me and I
> just had to organize. Although this poem did require more waiting
> than any others had ever before. I had to actually stop in the middle
> of writing to let some of the ideas settle down a bit, so I could find
> the stronger ones, like ". . . the quietest sound we know is air vent
> blowing, ear ringing silence" and "wind and hail hit us in our eyes
> like lead bass," or "the ebb of Earth's bass was keenly felt creeping
> through boots, penetrating and bouncing captivated souls." I found
> that writing in a form is just like writing free-verse, except that you
> have to be able to organize and manipulate what comes to you.

I read this reflection to the ninth graders. Some of them know Trevor as
a varsity football player. It helps. They need some writers to look up to who
aren't buried in the cemeteries of textbooks. I want them to hear him thinking on paper about how the writing happened, how he had to take his time
and listen—how the form wasn't just a puzzle to piece together, how he was
"found" by the ideas as he listened to the words.

And I want them to see him stretching and contracting the lines, playing
with the meanings of *bass/base*, using *rock* and *silence* as both nouns and
verbs, using *mountain* as a name to address.

"Here are some words to steal. Which ones came as surprises?"

They mention "the ebb of Earth's bass," "lead bass," "our souls were
insulated," "furious trees," "the sun's bass," "monster truck souls," "pimped
out" and "gremlin souls," "ear ringing silence"—"Is that a paradox?" someone
asks. Already they are starting to appreciate the suppleness of their language—that silence can be ear ringing; that nouns can also be verbs; that
puns (insulated soul, Earth's bass) can be serious; that literal can become
figurative; that together, *mountain* and *sole/soul* can make a mysterious and
fundamental music.

I had recently found a poem by Los Angeles poet Wanda Coleman in
which the poet Neruda is turned into a lowercase noun and repeated in a
variety of contexts, along with a sprinkling of Spanish words. It is exactly
the playful experimenting I want my students to try, so the next day, after
they share their new lists, we read Coleman's poem aloud several times:

## Neruda

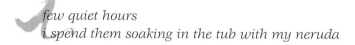few quiet hours
i spend them soaking in the tub with my neruda

in a dream a bearded moreno stranger
approaches me along a dark street in the plaza
as we pass he whispers hoarsely, "neruda"

on sunset boulevard a beggar accosts me
for spare change. i hand him my collected neruda

while my lover takes siesta i walk down to
the neighborhood bar for a game of pool solo. i order
dos besos. i put a quarter in the juke and notice
all selections read neruda

while standing in the supermarket checkout stand
i read tabloid headlines. one screams
"man force-feeds wife neruda"

(he tells me he is worried neruda is coming between us)

note found in cantonese fortune cookie:
neruda slept here[8]

The kids who know Spanish explain the one word the rest of us don't know and can't guess—*moreno*—and one of them mentions she has a book of Neruda's love poems. "I like how his name keeps turning up everywhere in this poem, like the author can't get away from him; he's always in her thoughts," she says.

Someone else comments on the sketchy sound of the lines: "It's so casual, like she's just making notes."

"Yes," I agree, "and I think part of what makes it seem casual is the lack of capital letters and punctuation. She uses punctuation only where she really needs it, to be clear, but the rest of the time you can figure out what she means. The line breaks help you, and so does reading it aloud."

Another student loves the way Coleman uses "neruda" to invent newspaper headlines and Chinese fortunes.

"Notice how most of the Spanish words in the poem are ones that have become part of our own language," I point out—"*plaza, siesta*—even *dos besos* you know if you read Hemingway stories. When do you think Spanish words and sounds started coming into American English?"

"Back with the explorers—like Cortez and that guy who was looking for the fountain of youth?" Jen suggests.

"And later with the cowboys along the Mexican border—and then all the migrant workers," Jake says.

"What are some of the cowboy words?" I ask them. And we make a list: *stampede, lasso, bronco, rodeo, lariat, mustang, desperado.* "When I was researching Billy the Kid, I read that the cowboys also picked up some pidgin English in dealing with Mexicans and Indians, like *no can do* and *long time no see.*

"And some of the Spanish themselves got words from the native cultures in the Caribbean—*chocolate, tomato, barbecue.* What Spanish words can you think of that we use all the time?"

"*Enchilada* and *tamales.* And *marijuana* sounds Spanish," Marissa says.

"So think about the foreign languages you know—even those you know just a few words of," I said. "Not just the one you're studying. . . . Now, can you think of someone you admire from one of those cultures, someone who speaks, or would have spoken, one of those languages you know a little bit of? Remember, Spanish-speakers live in a lot of places besides Spain—think of your favorite Latin American soccer players, and the Chicano culture in our own Southwest—Cesar Chavez was Chicano and so is poet Jimmy Santiago Baca. Remember there are countries in Africa where French is the official language. And think of all the famous people you studied in Ancient Civ. who spoke Latin. And you can certainly use Yiddish, if you know some. Now, by the end of the week, let's each write a poem about one of these people, using some words from their language. You can write the name in lowercase if you want—it might help you separate it from the person it refers to and make it easier for you to use it over and over in different stanzas and contexts. Try turning it into other parts of speech, too. Keep reading your lines aloud as you draft them, listening for the rhythms and reshaping if you don't like them. Remember, you can leave white space and use punctuation and line breaks to make the sounds and mood you want. As you draft, you'll discover whether the poem wants to be upbeat and jazzy, or lingering and reminiscent, and whether it needs to be skinny or move in and out like an accordion. Remember 'poetic license.' Remember how Trevor stretched some of the 'rules' for sestinas in order to express what he was feeling about climbing the mountain, and how unusual combinations of words 'found' him because he listened and waited."

At the end of the week, I invited volunteers to read their drafts aloud. "But first let's just go around the circle and hear the people whose names you chose to use." The list included Pushkin; Matisse; Mexican American actress Salma Hayek; Chavez the soccer player; Cortés; Oskar Schindler; Lou Diamond Phillips, a Filipino American actor; and Julius Caesar.

"Tell me something—did anyone end up writing a poem that wasn't really *about* the person whose name you were repeating?"

A number of hands went up. "Yeah," said one boy, "it got so the name was just a sound that I kept using—that I could do anything I wanted with. Kind of like a color in a painting."

As we listened to some of the poems, I noticed a new daring, a playfulness, and an attention to sound. Parker wrote:

### Chavez

> With quick and deadly precision
> a speeding chavez
> pierces the air,
> streaking to its target.
>
> Los diablos on the prowl,
> searing the midnight
> woods, searching,
> the only sound is from the screech owls,
> "Chaaaaavez, Chaaaaavez!"
>
> Noche en la ciudad,
> wolves howl at a chavez moon.
>
> Chavez brand liquor,
> seeping out a minute perforation,
> dripping out of the soul.

*Dos Equis,*
*the brand of choice*
*for an old Texan*
*with a chavez mustache.*

*Desperado on the scene,*
*luna miraba,*
*at first,*
*later,*
*the Sheriff*
*facedown in the dust,*
*smoke flowing out*
*the barrel of a .9 millimeter Chavez.*

*"Muy mal," replies the tired old man,*
*exiting*
*with a clink*
*of twin*
*chavez spurs.*

For the first time, I was hearing distinctive voices from almost everyone. From Kelly, who had just been on a field trip to the Holocaust Museum in Washington and who as a singer had experienced the sounds of many different languages, I heard a sensitivity to the music of both English and German:

### Die Nacht

*A room of silence is full of candles today.*
*The room is breathless and still*
*A presence of thousands is resting in this empty room.*
*It is possible to hear the low, soft whispering of their words.*

*I remember that day.*
*Die nacht, die kalte.*

*You are a dark and stern man,*
*Mr. Schindler.*
*Yet deeply rooted inside of you*
*is ein milteid fur das leben.*

*On that final night,*
*My heated tears stained my frozen cheeks.*
*Melting hearts.*
*We were all so solipsistic that night.*
*Lost someplace inside of ourselves*
*that had been hidden*
*for so long.*
*Someone had finally heard our forgotten screams.*

*I was just a girl.*
*too afraid to show you,*
*you have saved my people.*
*Slowly you have released mein welt.*

*"He who saves one, saves the world entire."*
*Mein gesamtes.*

*There is a room today,*
*it is breathless and still.*
*Liest hier mein speicher.*

Kelly had chosen not to repeat Schindler's name. She knew what she wanted to write about, and it wasn't exactly what Coleman had done with Neruda—but that was fine. I did argue with her about *solipsistic,* which she had collected earlier in her notebook. "It's acquired a negative coloration," I said. "Did you want that? I think you'll mislead any readers who are familiar with the word." But Kelly loved the sound, which she said was just right for the line.

A very quiet boy, who loved philosophical speculation and was reading *Moby Dick* with his father, turned out to have an impish sense of humor that I had been slow to recognize. I love the rhythm and puns of Ian's poem:

**Horatio**

I've got to go
To the airport, to
Sanz to a business viaje back in Chicago

Called a Taxi
Said "Take it slow"
Gave him a few extra Sanz

Baggage check bustle
"Any metal objects on you?"
Better take off my Sanz

Plane delays today
Wish I had una cosa to read
Think I'll buy a Sanz

Plane's arrived, I'm trying to board
"Sorry but you'll need to check that"
Sanz, I need my bag!

This is your captain speaking
In case of an aterrizaje forzoso
Please Sanz the flotation device located under your seat

Ah, Time to go to sleep
Catch some z's
Plenty of tiempo for Sanz later

I also love the ways in which Dmitri used sound in his Pushkin poem:

. . . . . . . . . . . .
A frustrated man runs a nervous hand through his hair
Mumbling, Pushkin.
He cautiously looks down the empty alley with hooded, dark eyes.
The pitter-patter of cat's paws in the shallow puddles

*Splish-splash-Pushkin!*

. . . . . . . . . . . .

*He pulls a door that won't budge.*
*The door reads, Pushkin!*
*The man forcefully pushkins his way through.*

Later, as the students wrote brief descriptions of how their poems had taken shape, Emilia explained that her "Matisse" poem

> came off of a dream, with a little edging from my memories of a Matisse exhibit as a child. I wanted to incorporate my feelings of awe at Matisse's drawings with the image of a new lover, and the awkward time before a new lover. When I wrote the poem, I was completely overwhelmed by the world around me and I felt lost in the shuffle of other people's every day lives. This sense of complete helplessness and the inability to control myself was also merged into the poem, as well as my limited French vocabulary.

I was struck by how many in the class had gone beyond what I'd expected—had not only discovered a playfulness in themselves that perhaps hadn't been tapped in a while, but had also found in this exercise a way to write about something important to them. I think the encouragement they'd been given to stretch the "rules," to taste the suppleness of language, may have freed them in other ways as well. What I loved most was the different kinds of music each voice was making. The last line of Emelia's poem says this best:

### L'art du café

*Sipping a cup of steaming Matisse*
*I look out the cafe windows*
*on to the bustling streets.*
*Les arbres sway in warm spring breezes*
*and the music runs circles around me.*
*Matisse turns around from the counter*
*his soft hands hitting the granite*
*like a water spider hits l'eau.*

*I watch him closely, studying his face.*
*I ask him to pour me another cup, s'il vous plait,*
*his customarily calm eyes scribble frantically,*
*he sees straight through me, he always can.*
*I can see him mumble "Matisse" under his breath.*
*I laugh and turn away regretfully, regarder,*
*I open my book and clumsily scratch*
*"Matisse" in the margins, note to self:*
*stop by the store on the way home*

*I scramble for my keys and try to open the door.*
*The metallic noises that come from the keys*
*remind me of summer days with my*
*Matisse, the scratching of our picnic plates.*
*I unlock the door to my apartment and*
*slip through dark Matisse mahogany.*
*I drop mes fleures, with their scent of nectar,*
*and pick up the mail.*
*The phone sonne "Matisse, Matisse."*

*He picks up the money from*
*the table and gives me change.*
*He drops a serviette on the rim of my glass,*
*it reads Matisse. I sit, silently,*
*and watch for a few minutes*
*the sharpness of his face, suddenly softer.*
*He watches back. He reaches out*
*and touches my hair, and we get up and sortir,*
*into the world that is suddenly ours.*

## Notes

1. E. E. Cummings, "since feeling is first," *Poems, 1923–1954* (New York: Harcourt, Brace, 1954), 208. This is a poet in whose lines students recognize a kindred need to rebel, even when they would be hard put to write a clear paraphrase of those lines, so it is unkind to turn their favorite poems into grammar lessons. But "anyone lived in a pretty how town" can trigger some lighthearted explorations of definite and indefinite (pronouns) by means of a

creative writing assignment in which the pronouns become characters; and the beautiful love poem "now all the fingers of this tree (darling)" can lead to some more than casual discussion of the adverbs on which the poem pivots— *now, then, never, forevering,* and *until.* Many of Cummings's poems offer fine examples of unusual and effective juxtapositions of words—and uses of individual words—that give us pause. And if student poets learn from Cummings to use too many parentheses, we must hope that this "now" is merely an "until."

2. Mark Twain, quoted by Robert McCrum, William Cran, and Robert MacNeil in *The Story of English* (New York: Viking Penguin, 1986), 47. This book is a companion to the PBS television series. Students need to know that the language they are learning to speak and write is the subject of an ancient and ongoing story. It is alive; it was born and continues to grow. Those of us who never read the story, who have picked up fragments of it over the course of our reading and teaching careers, can get a fuller picture from the PBS series and from this book, which takes a democratic and eclectic approach to the language. The two epigraphs, from Samuel Johnson and H. L. Mencken, both insist on the impossibility of preserving English from change, and Mencken actually celebrates change: "A living language is like a man suffering incessantly from small haemorrhages, and what it needs above all else is constant transfusions of new blood from other tongues. The day the gates go up, that day it begins to die." Chapter 9, "The New Englishes," and Chapter 10, "Next Year's Words," range over aboriginal Australia, South Africa, Jamaica, India, China, Hawaii, Alaska, California, Texas, and New York City.

3. McCrum, Cran, and MacNeil, *The Story of English,* 48.

4. McCrum, Cran, and MacNeil, *The Story of English,* 48.

5. Walt Whitman, quoted by Richard Lederer in *The Miracle of Language* (New York: Pocket Books, 1991), 206. Lederer's lively, entertaining books on language are great fun for browsing or reading cover to cover. They are full of games you can use with students and good for reading aloud in class. A former English teacher at St. Paul's School, a boarding school in Concord, New Hampshire, Lederer has a Ph.D. in linguistics but also a sense of humor (and an appalling capacity for punning) that must have helped him survive many a grammar lesson and now makes him a popular language commentator on National Public Radio. Of his books, *The Miracle of Language* is my favorite, as it reflects a passion for literature and history and offers numerous brief essays

on aspects of language that are fun to explore with students, ranging from
"The Case for Short Words," on which I have based many writing assignments
in poetry and prose, to "Is English Prejudiced?" and "One Word Can Change
the World." There are brief sections on Lewis Carroll, Shakespeare, Mark Twain,
T. S. Eliot, George Orwell, and lexicographers Dr. Samuel Johnson and Ambrose
Bierce.

6. McCrum, Cran, and MacNeil, The Story of English, 46.

7. Lederer, The Miracle of Language, 42

8. Wanda Coleman, "Neruda," reprinted in *Poets and Writers* (Sept./Oct. 1998),
49, from *Hand Dance* (Santa Rosa, CA: Black Sparrow Press, 1993).

# Chapter 8

# The Chimp Bit the Biologist, or Getting an Attitude

*I went to the animal fair.*
*The birds and the beasts were there.*
*The old baboon, by the light of the moon,*
*was combing his golden hair.*
*The monkey he got drunk,*
*and sat on the elephant's trunk.*
*The elephant sneezed, and fell to his knees,*
*but what became of the monk, the monk, the monk,*
*the monk?*

I hadn't thought of this song in years, but in typing the title of this chapter, I suddenly heard my mother's voice singing to me at bedtime. I suppose it's a kind of segue from the previous chapter and our playing with sound, or maybe a connection between foolery and drunken monkeys, but it also reminds me how I used to wonder, What *did* become of the monk? And then I would dreamily start inventing a story . . . until I drifted off to sleep.

Very young children tend to write very short stories—in very big letters. And the best way to draw them out, to find out more of those details that begin to create voice, or attitude, is to ask them questions: *Why did the monkey do that? And then what happened to him?* Now that my ninth graders had been given license to use words in unexpected ways, to plug foreign words into their writing, to stop worrying about being wrong, I thought we might be ready to work with the conventions, incorporating words from their notebook collections but stringing them together in a variety of traditional patterns. I also wanted the class to experience some frustration with these patterns—not just so they'd learn that editing is hard work and requires inventiveness, but so they'd understand better why many great writers of prose felt the need to innovate. I would show them Hemingway's fragments, created to express a dying man remembering; I'd let them hear how Alice Walker and Kaye Gibbons stretched language and syntax to create their young female characters' voices and crises. But we'd take a leaf from the first graders and start *small*.

So one day I write on the board, in very big letters, THE CHIMP BIT THE BIOLOGIST.

"This isn't yet a very interesting story," I tell the class. "For one thing, it doesn't have a tone of voice, an 'attitude.' But it's got potential. Think about the basic journalist questions: Which ones does it answer? . . . Okay, we've got *who* did *what* to *whom.* In terms of the parts of a sentence, the syntax, what have we got? . . . Right—subject, verb, and object. The basics. It's a pattern that's very familiar. If I'd written 'The bit chimp the biologist,' we'd have assumed first that 'bit' was describing 'chimp,' and we'd keep searching for a verb; but not finding one, we'd backtrack, assume 'bit' was the subject, and try to picture how a 'bit' might 'chimp' something. Of course, 'bit' *can* actually be a noun or verb, depending on where it's placed and how it's relating to the other words in the sentence, but when we move 'chimp' into the traditional verb place, I think our minds are almost willing to give up or its real meaning and twist it into a verb, maybe some new past tense of 'chip.' Meaning is a tricky thing in its relation to syntax—and so is the mind Dave Barry's mind led him to invent 'a family of words that grammarians call "metronomes," meaning "words that have the same beginning but lay eggs underwater."' [1] Whoever wants to invent a new element of grammar tonight, define it, and write some sample sentences gets extra credit. Anyway, we've got the basic story about this scientist and this chimp. What's missing?"

"When and where—the setting," says Jake. "Is it in the jungle, or is it in a lab?"

"Notice, though, how we already assume those are the likeliest possibilities," I say. "It could also be on a movie set, and the 'biologist' could be an actor. Or it could be in a cartoon. . . . But words do often evoke a little cluster of other words that are part of their 'world' in our minds. I read a sample sentence by Ron Padgett, from *Creative Reading*, in which he deliberately created blanks that offered *unfamiliar* cues: 'Santa Claus was dressed in his usual red b_____ and sported his traditional white z_____, around which were assembled the b_____s that pulled his d_____ through the sky.'[2] Padgett's given you a syntactical framework and included structures for adding description—for fleshing out a familiar image—but he's challenging most of your associations. It's almost as if this were a Santa Claus from a different culture or another planet. So you don't have to locate your chimp in a lab. What else is missing?"

"The how and the why," says Mark. "How did it happen, and why does it matter? What motivated the chimp, and who's more important to the story, him or the biologist? And what will this lead to?"

"If it's really a news article, it shouldn't have an opinion, should it?" asks Marissa. "Isn't reporting supposed to be objective—just the facts?"

"But nobody can be totally objective," Kelly argues.

"Well," I say, "if you were to read the same story in two different newspapers, you might get the same facts, but you might, depending on the papers, hear two different attitudes—maybe right off the bat in the way the headlines were written, and then in the particular quotes chosen from interviews, or in which facts were subordinated to others, or even in the coloration of some of the words. But let's think of our chimp episode as more of a story, or an editorial, maybe—less of a straight news report."

"We're going to try putting some flesh on this skeleton, build up some details. But I'm going to make a few specific requests." And I hand out a direction sheet:

> 1. Create an interesting moment—a miniature story—out of the situation in only *one* sentence. The sentence can be as long as you want.
>
> 2. Choose some interesting words from your and your partner's collections—we'll work in pairs—that will express your *attitude*

toward the situation, enough so your readers can pick up on it. Do you want us to find it funny? Do you want us to sympathize with the chimp or with the biologist, or with neither? Are you using the episode to argue against the use of animals in lab experiments? Is this the start of a fantasy—a horror story? Make the words express your attitude.

3. Use no more than one "and," and don't let your sentence become a run-on or comma splice. You can run it by me if you think you might be committing one of these grammatical sins. Remember that the colon and the semicolon can be helpful to you as a means of relating two ideas, and if you're not sure whether you're using one of them right, you can check that out with me, too.

Remember, as you attach details, they can take the form of whole phrases (prepositional to show when or where, or participial—-*ing* or -*ed* phrases) and clauses (the who, whose, which, and that clauses and the ones that tell how or how long or why). You don't have to know all these grammatical terms if your ear can do the job for you. Keep listening to your sentence as you add details. Don't just string adjectives—descriptive words—together: like "The huge, ornery, rebellious, dark-eyed chimp . . . ." Mark Twain wrote to a twelve-year-old boy, "When you catch an adjective, kill it. No, I don't mean utterly, but kill most of them—then the rest will be valuable. They weaken when they are close together. They give strength when they are wide apart."[3]

When I was in seventh or eighth grade, I remember, Miss Boland required us to write a book report of two pages with only one *and*. As I struggled and struggled, erasing and hurling balls of paper into the wastebasket, I wondered why she was making us do this. Now I see that she hoped I would end up with more interesting connections between ideas, more variety in sentence length and rhythm, and a growing awareness of the kinds of phrases and clauses at my disposal, even if I didn't yet know what their names were. I probably created plenty of run-on sentences.

Now, as I cruise around the computer room, I notice a lot of deleting, a lot of trial phrases and clauses: "On June 15 in a muggy, unpleasant lab on a meandering side-street on the Upper West side of New York City . . .";  "Because he wanted to get back to his jungle home in sultry Malaysia . . .";

"The chimp, a dangerous maverick specimen named . . ." I resolutely button my lip as dangling participles go up on the screens. The sky appears to be raining commas.

Jake calls me over to look at what he and Nick have gotten so far. "We have it down to this one long sentence, but I think it might be a run-on. Nick's not sure either."

I read aloud off the screen: "'On a frosty planet, where science had barely caught fire, the leering chimp maniacally bit the blithering biologist, who let loose a blizzard of curses when he felt the searing pain of the fangs sink into his metacarpus, but he had guts, he gave the chimp an oblique smile and continued to comb out the lice, while his wrist dripped blood onto his coat and a primitive mechanical device blasted his favorite song by the Apocalyptic Asteroids.'

"That's terrific! I love the words. I love the idea that this planet's so unscientific that all the biologist is doing is combing lice. I like the name of the band. I like the combination of 'frosty'—literal frost—and 'blizzard of curses'—a metaphorical blizzard there. You clearly want me to look down my nose at the planet, admire the biologist's cool, and see the chimp as some horror flick monster. So there's plenty of attitude. I think you could use a colon to fix the run-on. Where could you put it? Remember, a colon signals that an example is coming up, something that expands and clarifies the statement that was just made. It's a pretty dramatic punctuation mark."

"How about if we put it right after 'but he had guts'?"

"Perfect."

This team has a better instinct for syntax—or perhaps more varied reading experience—than some of the others, and arrived at their "story" more easily. On another screen, I read: "The chimp was gigantic and was named Anthony, it bit the octogenarian biologist right on his nose, a warty excrescence, which surprised his menage a trois, at twilight he went home for dinner, they asked him what happened and he explained that this half-assed biped . . ."

"You've got some fascinating words here. I love *warty* and *excrescence*—though a wart *is* an excrescence, so you don't need both of them. *Twilight*'s one of my favorite words, very romantic, I love the echo of the two long *i* sounds, but it doesn't particularly fit with the *tone—the attitude*—of 'half-assed biped' or 'warty excrescence.' It's great that you know the French—*ménage à trois.* And 'half-assed biped' is a good insult. But none of these words help me figure out what the writers' attitude—your attitude—to the event is. I get the biologist's attitude all right! But can we assume the writers feel the same way? Then the other thing I notice is that you've run one statement right into another into another into another, with no words or punctuation to relate one fact to the next *or* to separate them—except for *which*. So you've got a pretty gigantic run-on sentence—lots of individual sentences spliced with commas. Have you read it aloud yet? . . . Okay, do that a few times; both of you read to one another exactly the way it's punctuated on the screen, and listen hard. If this were a story being remembered from a long time back, just pieces of it drifting through someone's mind, you know, the way thoughts drift, you might *want* to run things together like this—and that would be fine—but there's no evidence in your word choices to suggest that you're trying to do this."

By the end of the period, most pairs have created an attitude and have edited out at least some of their run-together clauses. We've had time to hear some pieces read aloud in order to identify which words help us recognize the writers' attitude, and we've put a couple of problem sentences on the overhead projector and fixed them—with "relating" or "subordinating" words, as the class is starting to call them, or with semicolons and colons. (In using terminology with ninth graders, I think fondly of Dave Barry's invented term, the *collaborative inductive*: "Grammatically, 'happen' is a collaborating inductive that should be used in predatory conjunctions such as: 'Me and Norm would like to buy you two happening mamas a drink.'" He has also created the *corpuscular phrase* and the *antibody*.)[4]

The sentence about Anthony the gigantic chimp has been recast, with the help of several subordinators, some new adjectives, and a semicolon: "Because he had been starved for a week, Anthony, the ravenous chimp, bit the crazy biologist right on his warty nose; in his paranoia the octogenarian injected him with a fatal venom, and, since this had happened too many times already, the animal rights groups lobbied successfully to close down the lab."

Next day we return to our reading of Kaye Gibbons's novel *Ellen Foster*, written in the voice of an eleven-year-old girl whose late mother had been abused by an alcoholic husband. After her mother's death, Ellen not only has to fend for herself but also has to fend off her father's abuse. The novel is set in the South, so we're getting a few regionalisms—"I aim to," "right much"—and we're also hearing some of the confusions typical of children—"romantic fever" for rheumatic fever, "wa-la" for voila, etc. But what's most striking are the ways Ellen, as narrator of her own story, leaps back and forth from past to present, sometimes with no obvious links, and how her thoughts run together when she's remembering painful moments. Sometimes the language is so visceral that it's as though her whole body—and the writer's body—is actually reliving those moments.

After listening to the class discuss certain passages they had marked the night before, I suggest, "Let's look at this passage where Gibbons has Ellen tell you about escaping from her father that night when all the men have been drinking with him. How does it make you feel—and what is there in the writing that makes you feel this way, do you think?"

> You get out before one can wake up from being passed out on your floor. You get out before they start to dream about the honey pie and the sugar plums. Step over the sleeping arms and legs of dark men in shadows on your floor. You want to see a light so bad that it comes to guide you through the room and out the door where a man stops you and the light explodes into a sound that is your daddy's voice.
>
> Get away from me he does not listen to me but touches his hands harder on me. That is not me. Oh no that was her name. Do not oh you do not say her name to me. That was her name. You know that now stop no not my name.
>
> I am Ellen.
> I am Ellen.
>
> He pulls the evil back into his self and Lord I run. Run down the road to Starletta. Now to the smoke coming out of the chimney against the night sky I run.
>
> Down the path in the darkness I gather my head and all that is spinning and flying out from me and wonder oh you just have to wonder what the world has come to.[5]

Before we started reading this novel together, I discussed the subject of abuse with the class. We read a poem that one of my older students had written some years ago about having been abused by her father (which she'd allowed me to use as long as I kept it anonymous), and we talked about reasons why this happens, stories we'd read or heard about it, local shelters for battered women and children, treatment available for the abused and the abuser, the word *victim* versus the word *survivor.* We talked about how and why a mother might abuse her child, and whether we could imagine ourselves reaching a state in which we might turn violent on someone we cared for. The school psychologist came in to discuss the state law about reporting abuse and the question of confidentiality. And I explained to the class that students who found themselves uncomfortable as we read or discussed the book should see me—that we could arrange independent study of a different book, as is sometimes done at the college level. One year I had a student who I knew had been abused, so her mother and I and her advisor agreed that the girl and I would look at this particular passage together and she would decide whether she wanted to read the book or not. She ended up choosing to read it but asking that she be allowed to leave the room if a class discussion began to feel painful. I think she left just once. It seems to help that Ellen is such a feisty, independent child and finds herself a warm and caring foster mother. In fact, the way the book is structured, she's already with her "new mama" when she starts telling about the past, and she keeps interrupting the story to describe what her new life is like—which is reassuring.

After we've heard the passage about Ellen's father read aloud, there's a long silence. Words sitting on a page seldom register in the same way as when they are "given voice," even though our minds "hear" them as we read to ourselves. Eventually some hands go up.

"Whose name is he saying?" Ted asks.

"Her mother's name, isn't it?" Brittany offers.

"It was confusing the first time I read it because of the way the sentences run together. But when Marissa read it aloud, it was much clearer. And I think the confusion is good, because that's how Ellen must have felt, and actually that's how the father probably was, too, because he's drunk and he's mixing her up with her mother."

"What's that light she sees? Is that a real light?"

"Oh, I didn't think about that. But it probably isn't because it 'explodes' into her father's voice when he stops her at the door. I think it's just her instinct that helps her find her way through the room."

"I like the last sentence where everything's spinning and flying out of her. It's like she's being blown apart and she's trying to hold her life together and who she is."

"Yes," I agree. "It's very physical—the running out of the house and the movement of things flying out of her at the same time. And then her wondering 'what the world has come to.' That 'oh'—you're not expecting it in the middle of the sentence—seems to come right from the gut. The words and the chaos of the sentence structure really do make me feel that it's not just

Ellen's father but the whole world that's gone wrong when something like this can happen."

"I like the way she mixes the 'you' and the 'I' together," Alex observes. "That's kind of confusing, too, but it makes me feel like she's talking to me, like she's telling me personally this story about what happened to her. And it makes her sound kind of mixed up and panicked."

"I still don't like that she never uses quotation marks."

"Oh, I got used to that. It makes you remember that Ellen's the one telling the story and it's all in her head. It's all her voice, really—everybody else who talks is just her telling us what they said."

"I like the way she puts 'I am Ellen' all by itself on the line and then repeats it on the next line. It makes you hear how important that is—how desperate she feels. I didn't know you could do that—make a paragraph just be one line—except when you're writing dialogue."

"The way all the words rush together makes it kind of feel like a dream, a nightmare."

"So you think Gibbons gets away with breaking some rules here?" I ask them. "Is she taking a risk, doing that?"

"Yeah, she's risking that we'll be confused—but I think it's worth it," Brittany says. "It's not as confusing as E. E. Cummings, anyway."

"Could you do it in journalism?" I ask them.

"No, people read a newspaper to get the facts," Tom says. "They want to hear which team won and what plays different guys made. Or what the Serbs are doing. You don't need to know how people feel about things. And you don't want to be confused."

"Well," I say, "there was a development back in the sixties called the New Journalism, where writers like Tom Wolfe and Hunter S. Thompson and Norman Mailer (who was a novelist to start with, anyway) and Jimmy Breslin and others started writing in a much more personal style, with a lot of attitude and very colloquial language and rhythm—about surfers in California and political campaigns and the Mafia and so on. They wrote articles—actually more for magazines than newspapers—and they also wrote book-length pieces. And then there're the columnists—well, you know, the school paper has a humor columnist and someone who writes reviews of rock concerts—and their styles are pretty personal and unconventional by news reporting standards. The *New York Times* has regular columnists on the op-ed page who offer their own interpretations of a situation or issue, and sometimes they might use fragments—for dramatic effect or to sound conversational. But you're right, in general journalists don't stretch the conventions as much as, say, novelists and poets. You should read some Tom Wolfe, though. You'd like his voice. The first of his books I read was *The Electric Kool-Aid Acid Test.*"

And we go back to *Ellen Foster.*

Next day, to provide another example of a voice that was achieved by breaking with conventions, I bring in a passage from Hemingway's story "The Snows of Kilimanjaro."

"In this story," I tell them, "a writer is dying of gangrene out in the African bush, and he's remembering all the parts of his life that he never wrote stories about. The way Hemingway put these memories in italics helps me keep them separate from the rest of the story, but he also put the words together in ways that make me feel what it's like to remember things from long ago in my own life. Let's read this passage aloud, but I think we'll also each try typing it out. That's another way to slow down and get the feel of the writing—of how it's put together."

> *No, he had never written about Paris. Not the Paris that he cared about. But what about the rest that he had never written? . . .*
>
> *About the half-wit chore boy who was left at the ranch that time and told not to let any one get any hay, and that old bastard from the Forks who had beaten the boy when he had worked for him stopping to get some feed. The boy refusing and the old man saying he would beat him again. The boy got the rifle from the kitchen and shot him when he tried to come into the barn and when they came back to the ranch he'd been dead a week, frozen in the corral, and the dogs had eaten part of him. But what was left you packed on a sled wrapped in a blanket and roped on and you got the boy to help you haul it, and the two of you took it out over the road on skis, and sixty miles down to town to turn the boy over. He having no idea that he would be arrested. Thinking he had done his duty and that you were his friend and he would be rewarded. He'd helped to haul the old man in so everybody could know how bad the old man had been and how he'd tried to steal some feed that didn't belong to him, and when the sheriff put the handcuffs on the boy he couldn't believe it. Then he'd started to cry. That was one story he had saved to write. He knew at least twenty good stories from out there and he had never written one. Why?[6]*

I listen to the sound of the computers as everybody types out the passage. Most mornings before school I copy into my notebook favorite lines from whatever poet I happen to be reading, partly to warm up for writing something of my own, but also to slow down and hear the music through my fingers, to see the words taking shape letter by letter and the syntax of the line word by word. Ron Padgett, in *Creative Reading*, describes what he learned from typing an entire collection of Ted Berrigan's poems:

> Typing Ted's poems made me realize that their basic unit of construction was less the clause or phrase than single words placed side by side ("like bricks," as he put it). I also noticed that he favored words that had a weightiness, a physical presence. Words like "shackled," "frolicsome," "unabridged," and "Berrigan." This vocabulary gave the work a certain heft, which he kept from being burdensome by means of the light melody of vowels that played in and out. Using the carriage return, I was also able to focus more clearly on the way he used line breaks, and how these affected the momentum of the entire work.[7]

"So what are you noticing?" I ask my typists.

"Well, the words are really simple. There's nothing I'd steal for my notebook, except maybe *haul.* I like the sound of that," Katie says. "And *corral.* You could use that as a noun *or* a verb."

"The simple words—that's what he's famous for, isn't it?" Jon asks. "This real streamlined style—nothing extra. I like it. Nothing gets in the way—you feel the cold and the beating; you hear the rifle shot."

"Yes, and he tells you the boy's a half-wit and the old man's a bastard. There's nothing to guess."

"But he makes me feel very sad for the boy," says Katie. "It's not like we're meant to sneer. It's kind of like Lennie in *Of Mice and Men*. It's when the boy starts to cry. Or maybe when he says the boy went all that way thinking he'd be rewarded and that the guy was his friend. That's so harsh. I hate it when you go along thinking somebody likes you and then they do something so you know they never really cared at all."

"Yeah, I know. That's just what I was thinking about when I read this part," I agree. "Actually, I was reliving the moment, years ago, when I went into my boss's office thinking I was going to be given a raise, but instead I was being laid off because the school was losing money. I can still feel the shock. But did you notice any odd sentences?"

"Do you mean where he starts using 'you' all of a sudden? That kind of surprised me."

"Yes, because he'd said 'when *they* came back to the ranch,' and then suddenly he lets us know that he's part of the 'they.' The boy goes on being 'he,' and then at the end, the narrator refers to himself as 'he.' Pronoun shifts can be tricky. Was it confusing?"

"Nope."

"What I was noticing when I typed this myself were a couple of real long sentences with lots of 'ands,' just piling things up as he remembers them, and the fourth sentence—'The boy refusing and the old man saying he would beat him again.' Technically, that's a fragment. Just those two *-ing* participial phrases. And later, too: 'He having no idea that he would be arrested. Thinking he had done his duty. . . .' Are those fragments confusing?"

"I didn't notice they weren't regular sentences," Alex says. "But I think they just make it sound like the writer is remembering—you know, the way thoughts just stream along, sort of out of control, the way memories come back. And maybe if this guy is supposed to be dying, it helps show that he's losing control in a way—that he won't be able to make a story out of this memory. I guess writing down something that happened would be a way of getting hold of it, reshaping it."

"So this is something you could try," I suggest. "Hemingway and Gibbons are both using pretty basic words but putting them together in unusual ways that make you feel things are out of control. They've risked confusing us a little in order to create voices for characters who are in frightening situations, or are remembering a frightening situation. They're not just reporting the facts of the situation—it's not just 'The chimp bit the biologist'—but they're using words and syntax together to make you feel what the speaker feels. Let's try tonight to write a paragraph in the voice of someone who's in a disturbing situation—and let the word order and patterns risk confusion. Say 'oh' right in the middle of a sentence if you need to. Let the sentences go 'spinning and flying' so we 'just have to wonder what the world has come to.'"

## Notes

1. Dave Barry, "English, As It Were," in *Dave Barry Talks Back,* 200 (see note 5, chap. 2).

2. Ron Padgett, *Creative Reading: What It Is, How to Do It, and Why* (Urbana, IL: National Council of Teachers of English, 1997), 52. Poet, translator, and director of publications at Teachers & Writers Collaborative, Padgett brings a diverse background and a lively sense of humor to bear on the "miracle that is reading." He asks us to take a fresh look at the printed page and to approach the teaching of reading with the same imagination we bring to the teaching of creative writing. The book is not about teaching beginners to read but rather "for people who have learned to read—perhaps even well—in conventional ways, but who sense a creeping staleness in their reading." It demonstrates ways "to make reading more flexible, various, and imaginative," and assumes that reading and writing are two sides of the same coin, not each a cluster of disparate skills and drills. Padgett argues that if we teach children to read mainly so they can get a "higher" score or a "better" job, "we forget "the warmth of learning about the world, other people, and oneself, of learning to live more fully and variously, with greater understanding, clarity, and compassion, as well as beauty and good humor" (xv). The book offers some inventive exercises for creative reading in ways that blend reading and writing and that make room for "the joys of misunderstanding"; a discussion of the influence of typography, movies, and television on reading; and advice on the creating and reading of comic strips and calligrams. It's dedicated, suitably, to Kenneth Koch, and its epigraphs range from "The Song of Solomon" to Grouch Marx.

3. Mark Twain, in a letter to a twelve-year-old boy, quoted in Lederer, *The Miracle of Language,* 128 (see note 5, chap. 7).

4. Dave Barry, "Punctuation 'R Easy," in *Dave Barry Is Not Making This Up* (New York: Fawcett Columbine/Crown, 1994), 216.

5. Kaye Gibbons, *Ellen Foster* (New York: Vintage Books, 1990), 37–38.

6. Ernest Hemingway, "The Snows of Kilimanjaro," in *The Snows of Kilimanjaro and Other Stories* (New York: Scribner, 1955), 22–23.

7. Padgett, *Creative Reading,* 106.

# Chapter 9

# Words in the News

THE LIMITS OF MY LANGUAGE ARE THE LIMITS OF MY MIND. ALL I KNOW
IS WHAT I HAVE WORDS FOR.

LUDWIG WITTGENSTEIN[1]

The first year I taught tenth grade the curriculum included three weeks of studying the *New York Times*. Great bundles were delivered to the school every day, and if you had a first-period class, you tried to get to school early so you could skim and prep. Don Roberts, my mentor, would stick his head around the corner to warn, "The science section's all physics—you'll love it!"

I'd groan, so to cheer me up he'd add, "But there's a great Russell Baker." It didn't matter what Baker was writing about. Don meant that the column contained some Great Words that we could teach. "My word of the day," Don might say, "is *gumption*. Baker used it three times. It's got a remarkable derivation. Know where it comes from?" I hadn't a clue, and I hadn't yet learned that Don enjoyed inventing—words, derivations, quotations, literary critics. Sometimes he'd give his students an essay topic based on a "famous quotation"—his own current theory on, say, characterization—and attribute it to a wholly imaginary expert, preferably one with three names.

"Yes," Don would continue, "*gumption*'s closely related to *gumshoe*—you know, those rubber-soled shoes that the slang for *detective* comes from. *Gumshoe* derives from an old Cherokee word for 'extra soft moccasins.' If an Indian spy succeeded in sneaking up and checking out a group of white settlers without their knowing it, he was praised for his *gumshoen*. You want to be sure and tell the kids about this one."

Gradually I acquired caution. And learned not only to question authorities but, on occasion, to invent them. Growing up female in the 1950s, with my father on the school faculty, was not the best recipe for deviltry. I loved the praise I earned for trying to please my teachers. I was a "highly motivated" reader with great respect for anything in print, wrote the longest and tidiest papers in the class, and was an expert at following directions. When in turn I became a teacher, I assumed that all good students were like my younger self. Much as I valued Don, it took me years to realize that his love of mischief and rebellion was a quality to search out and value in students. Recently I was reading Tom Romano's description of himself writing in "double voice" along with his students during an essay test. In the left-hand column, he writes his thoughts about Thoreau and "Civil Disobedience." In the right-hand column, he writes, "Oh, Jesus, Thoreau—what a conceited ass. He's badgered me for two weeks. I shoulda read them essays!" Romano speculates that this second voice is "George, the smart, likable, hulking wag, sitting in the last seat in the row by the windows." But then he realizes that "both voices were mine, the one on the right the sixteen-year-old Tom who still lives in me."[2] As I read this, I realized, with a certain admission of envy, that my sixteen-year-old self wouldn't have sounded remotely like the hulking wag in the back row whose mind I've had such trouble getting into all year. While I don't want to place overmuch importance on gender, I know that reading the work of men who approach art, life, and kids in this spirit of mischief and disregard for authority—Ron Padgett, for example, and Kenneth Koch and Tom Romano, and, yes, Dave Barry—has enlarged my horizons.

So now when I use newspapers in the classroom, I start with the idea that of course we don't have to believe every word we read in them. Nor do we have to read the articles in the order of importance that the *Times* has dictated. I had a wonderful English teacher in high school who assigned us the first eight pages of the Book Review section every week, and ever since, I've started my Sunday mornings with that; I rarely start with the first page. I like Ron Padgett's idea of encouraging kids to paste together a new front page made from the sections and articles *they* like to read first. [3]

For the classroom, I've developed a method of distilling articles into word clusters, which can then be performed aloud. Students work in pairs or small groups, choosing an article from among, say, five that I've picked for general interest and language possibilities. As they skim it, they copy down words and brief phrases that seem to capture the essence of the piece and its voice—its tone and meaning, its sounds and images. Then they present their collection of words to the class, using movement and voices and, if they wish, crayons and mural paper.

I remind them that "meaning" isn't simply drawn from facts but from the facts' effect on the reader—that the meaning Marissa takes away may be different from Jake's. I mention that knowledge has to do with the heart and limbs and nerves as well as the head. And I urge them to use their dictionaries to look up any words they can't guess from the context.

When I look through today's *New York Times,* Tuesday, July 13, 1999, I see a promising headline in the Science section—"A History: When the State Uses People as Guinea Pigs." As I skim, I build a word cluster: *old as arrogance and cruelty, genetic warfare, bubonic pandemic, curiosity piqued, declassified secrets, a parade of horribles, ingest suspect bacteria, injecting plutonium, bombarded with chemical weapons, infertility drugs, sick from fava beans.* (I could simply give this list to a class and ask them what they think the article's about: Make up a headline.) I'm drawn to the imagery—a parade, a bombardment. The idea of a parade of horribles is startling, almost a paradox, given our usual associations with parades; and the use of *horrible* as a noun is striking. We'd normally expect *horrors; horribles* stops us in our tracks. Both are rooted in the very physical Latin *horrere*—to bristle with fear; *horrid* used to mean bristling and rough, and the image of injecting plutonium into a human being, do give me an almost physical reaction. My ears pick up on certain rhythms—"bubonic pandemic"—and the assonance of "old as arrogance." I think about what my students would learn from tracking down the derivation of *pandemic*—and *pandemonium* (a quick visit to *Paradise Lost*), *panacea, pantheism, panorama, PanHellenic, Pan-America.* The frequent coupling of *pique* with *curiosity* is also interesting—as though one's curiosity lies slumbering until something pricks it into action. *Pique,* like horror, is one of those metaphorical words whose abstract meaning retains the shadow of its physical origins: *pique* from the French *piquer,* to prick, and Latin *piccare,* to pick: "cf. pickax, pike." I know my history buffs would want to discuss the "bubonic plague"—and probably the issue of "declassifying secrets." We might also note how from being used in labs, *guinea pig* has become a term for any subject of any sort of experiment. And we'd certainly end up talking about the concept of "genetic warfare."

I turn to the Arts section and find two good possibilities. First, with my particular clientele in mind, I skim an account of the postponed season finale of *Buffy the Vampire Slayer*, headlined "Saving the Graduates from Being Eaten." I underline *deathbed, poisoned arrow, eating spiders, student massacre, Sunnydale High, blood-red caps and gowns, conflagration, adult idiocy, repartee, verbal delight, wielding swords, flaming arrows, fantasy premise, battling demons, Trenchcoat Mafia*. I also pause to enjoy the rhythm of a sample of dialogue from the show—the comic effect of each line getting shorter—and ponder why the word *hummus* should crack me up:

> Cordelia: I personally don't think it's possible to come up with a crazier plan.
>
> Oz: We attack the mayor with hummus.
>
> Cordelia: I stand corrected.

Then, in a different key, "Real Wind Breezes in to Bolster Its Image"—a review of a new Trisha Brown dance at Jacob's Pillow, a summer dance center in the Berkshires: *real wind, breezes, sweet wind, gusted, fresh, green woods, romp, playful, exuberant, release, five flowing, giddy, feinting, falling, piling, wheeling, happy scrawl, slippery feet, bound and chatter, blithe, hot and cool, glisten*. I can visualize a student group handling these words, perhaps the bravest student trying out some of the moves while the others chant the words, and then everyone layering the adjectives and verbs, at different pitches and paces, and scrawling them in green on the wall. We could talk a bit about this modern dance vocabulary, all the seemingly everyday movements—romp, fall, pile, wheel, feet chattering and bounding—that a choreographer, scrawling on dancers' bodies, can make into art, as opposed to the ballet tradition of exotic, beautiful but impossible (for most of us), gravity-defying movements with French names: arabesque, fouetté, piquet turn, tour jeté. We could marvel together at the challenge of finding words to describe the patterns of moving bodies. Would it be any easier to translate the moves of a ball game or a soccer match into words? We could talk about feinting—as a boxing or fencing technique, as pretense and as play. We could scrawl and sprawl.

From dance it's an easy jump to the Sports section. Or it should be. Whenever I read the sports pages—which, unless there's tennis news, I have to push myself to do, in the name of all my student athletes—I think of my friend Don Roberts idolizing Red Smith, the sportswriter, and his insistence that I could learn about good writing by subscribing to *Sports Illustrated*. Normally I get my kicks by reading Dave Barry's humor columns on why baseball statistics matter more to guys than do the names and ages of their children. But today I skim articles on two ball players, Hideki Irabu of the New York Yankees and Pedro Martinez of the Boston Red Sox. I've developed the habit of reading the sports writing in our school paper, on the lookout for students who can write well about what they love—which may not happen to be *Macbeth* or *The Scarlet Letter*. I clip, photocopy, and read aloud classroom sets of the best student sports writing, and we study it as carefully as if it were a sonnet by Keats to see how the language works. Today I recognize the usual energetic lingo—*fast ball popping, curve ball, changeup, fired, smack, throwing lights out, snare, splitter, slammed, hammered his three-run homer.* I admire a couple of sentences describing how a hitter must react to a fast pitch:

> [Y]ou must prepare to swing quickly, cocking your hands for the explosive movement of the bat; there is only an instant to discern whether Martinez has thrown a fast ball, curve ball, or changeup. The hitter's weight begins to shift from back to front, his bat is moving forward, the swing reaching the point of no return—and all too often, that is when they realize that Martinez has thrown a changeup low and out of the strike zone, or that he has spun a curve ball.

I can visualize this scene, feel it in my body, not just because of the words but because of the shift in verb tense: "begins to shift," "is moving forward," "reaching," then the dash and the dramatic rhythm it creates—"that is when they realize." I like even better hearing his teammates describe Martinez's deceptive approach to pitching:

> He just sort of slings the ball, like a rubber band. . . . His arm and motion is just so free and easy. . . . He has that real easy cheese, that easy fast ball. He's not an intimidating guy as far as size. He's not like Randy Johnson, or like Kerry Wood, who's got all those

body parts coming at you. Pedro is nice and loose and—*wap!*—he's
on you. You know he throws hard, but he's sneaky.

*Easy cheese*—great sound, so relaxed it's funny, lulling you into a false sense
of security, just the way Martinez's looseness does. I love the picture of "all
those body parts coming at you"—as though they're on a movie screen,
getting bigger and closer. Because the articles about both ball players offer
character sketches and personal histories, we get some of the words we're
more used to finding in the Book Review section: *braggadocio, retrospect,
pedestrian, viable, jeopardize, incensed, imminent, brawl, branded, grittily,
scoffed, destiny*—a collection typical, in its origins from Old English, French,
and Latin, of the basic mix that is English. *Brawl* from Middle English—to
raise a clamor; *braggadocio*, with its Italian flavor, from a character in
Spenser's chivalric epic *The Faerie Queene* (1590s); *retrospect*, with its idiom,
*in retrospect*, and its useful Latin roots—"backward" and "look"—which
spawned *speculation, auspicious, spectrum, perspicacious, circumspect, respite,
specious; scoff*, with its connections to early Danish (*skuf, skof*—mockery)
and its use as slang, *to scoff*—to eat voraciously (today my students "scarf"
down their lunch)—and, starting in the 1920s, its connection to *scofflaw*—
anyone who flouts (not flaunts) the law, especially one who fails to pay
fines owed; and *jeopardize*, from the Old French *j(e)upartie*, literally, divided
play, hence, uncertain chance, hence the kids' favorite classroom game of
Jeopardy.

On the editorial page, I find "Considering the View from Summer's
Road," a mild satire of the typical family summer trip into the wild: *minivan,
pullout, video camera, hoodoos, raven, bristlecone pines, unintelligible vastness,
vista, plastic tomahawks, SnoKones, perplexing, white-legged, subdivision of
RV's, Chieftain, Conquest, Eagle, microwaves, web of familiarity, chain experiences, hidden fear, limits of known world, democratize the sublime, souvenirs,
purveyors, unknown country.* It is interesting to see how the language falls
into two contrasting groups till finally *democratize the sublime* brings both
together in an uneasy alliance. This is a piece that could easily get us
started reminiscing aloud and on paper about our own family vacations. It
could also lead us into reading and writing haiku, with their two, sometimes
contrasting images and their invitation to enter a moment. Or into a discussion of the image making of car advertisers, whose *Eagles* and *Chieftains*
usually spend their days parked in suburban shopping malls.

Articles from the Science section are particularly useful for getting experience with analogies. And I don't mean primarily as practice for the verbal SAT, but as a technique for making the esoteric more accessible. The *Times* science writers realize they are writing for the layperson. In today's issue, almost all the writers start out with an analogy to something familiar, or at least with an allusion that most of their readers are likely to recognize. The piece that asks whether doctors are losing touch with hands-on medicine begins with a biblical allusion: "In the beginning—before, that is, the chest X-ray, the CAT scan, the transesophageal echocardiogram, the prostate-specific antigen, the thalium stress test and the gadolinium-enhanced MRI—was the physical examination." It moves on to make a comparison between all these tests with the hard names and the physical exam, which it says was, up until recently, "medicine's most elegant diagnostic tool." "Tool" brings the subject down to the everyday. Five paragraphs later the image returns, underlining the physicality, the manual nature, of the tool by introducing the idea of rust: "If you have available technology as an alternative, you're going to rust at the bedside." The young, examining doctors—their inexperienced hands and ears—are the tools, but for want of practice, they are getting rusty.

A brief column on new discoveries about how bees stay on course begins with an analogy to airplane pilots: "Flying a plane in crosswinds can be tricky. The pilot has to compensate for the wind's speed and direction, changing the plane's heading accordingly. If it's tough for a plane, imagine what it must be like when a tiny bumblebee is buffeted by a crosswind." And an article titled "Monkey See, Monkey Do: Brain's Path from Sight to Action" starts off with a slightly vague analogy between the brain's operation of moving an arm to answer the phone and an Avon Lady's plan for meeting her sales goals.

The Book Review offers the weekly list of bestsellers, which is fun to look at and to rewrite with one's own current favorites, but it also provides students with many words useful for talking and writing about the literature they're reading in and out of class—words that describe and analyze character, structure, and tone, words that make judgments. It's helpful for those students whose first love is not books to discover that sports, science, computer, music, fashion, food, and movie columns all have their own vocabularies for describing and assessing their subjects, just as the book review has. And that writers in all those areas use similar techniques in stringing together their words—recreating specific instances, drawing comparisons, making analogies, using allusions, generalizing from examples, offering opinions, and throughout, consciously and unconsciously, creating a voice that expresses an attitude toward the material.

The typical newspaper book review is rarely as esoteric or scholarly as the literary criticism students may run into, but it will usually offer them some unfamiliar, often abstract, language. Skimming a review of *Warp Speed: America in the Age of Mixed Media,* I collected: *assert, provocative, disperse, unsparing, strident, supplanted, attribute, wallow, gleeful, castigate, premise, pivotal, incontrovertible, disseminate, scant, imminent, pundit, metamorphose, voracious, zeal, scooped* (the journalistic term), *demise, innuendo, episode, dispassionate, deconstruction, plight,* and—my favorite—*pablum.* (Yes, a lot of SAT words here.) These are not words that lend themselves to clustering by subject or mood, and some of them are not easy to act out, though the range of sounds is enticing. The other problem is that many may be unfamiliar to students and hard to guess from context—and students will not enjoy looking up all twenty-eight. At this juncture, I remind myself that I do not have to "teach" all these words. They'll turn up again, if not this month, then next year. I am not single-handedly responsible for making each student a complete master or mistress of the English language. (I do like, by the way, the term *Webmistress;* it reminds me of the girl harpist in Anne McCaffrey's *Dragonsinger* series.) We can choose a couple of words we especially like the *sound* of—*pundit,* for example (and *punditry*), with its Hindu and Sanskrit derivations from a word for "learned man." Or *gleeful.* (I'm suddenly remembering humorist Richard Armour's statement about Lady Macbeth: "She rubbed her hands with glee—a Scottish detergent of the time.") We could choose a couple of words that have useful roots, each of which might teach us ten more words: *provocative, disseminate, metamorphose, voracious,* or *deconstruct.*

Or we could choose *pablum,* the taste and texture of which I vividly remember from infancy—surprising how blandness can hold a place in the memory—but whose primary association is with a classmate in high school Latin class who translated a line from Caesar's *Gallic Wars* to the effect that the horses were turned loose in the field to graze on pablum (*pabulum* was the Latin word for food). This was Sandy, a guy I used to dance with, who talked primarily about hunting and fishing; he grew up to be a terrific vet.

If one is faithful enough to the newspaper of one's choice, from time to time an article will pop up that works perfectly in conjunction with a particular book or lesson one is about to teach. We probably all have a yellowing

file of such articles; those of us who began teaching before the photocopy
machine arrived on the scene may even have a purpling file. One of my two
favorites—no, three favorites, if I count the plot outline of *Oedipus Rex* told
in license plates—is a series called "Children of the Shadows" from the
*Times* some years ago, weekly interviews done by college students who had
spent a week or more talking with an underprivileged teenager about his or
her life.[4] The other is a review of several modern dance pieces choreo-
graphed by Paul Taylor that focused on their checkered tone, their emotional ambivalence.

   "Children of the Shadows" became a project for my ninth graders: to
create and present monologues in the voices of these teenagers. I paired it
with the voices of children from Robert Coles's fifth volume of *Children in
Crisis,* about kids whose parents were extremely rich.[5] This project not only
focused my students on voice, both written and spoken, and encouraged
them to enter into the lives of teenagers in circumstances quite different
from their own, but it also made a bridge from the character and situation of
Holden Caulfield—which felt fairly familiar—to those of Ellen Foster, which
didn't. I discovered as we worked with these life stories that sheltered and
mostly privileged fourteen-year-olds put a high premium on a story being
"true to life"; they want to know what is "out there," and they can't quite
trust J. D. Salinger's version of it or Kaye Gibbons's version of it since these
are novels. Hearing the actual words of actual kids and recognizing that
these kids share some of the attitudes of the two fictional characters we are
reading about seems to validate the fiction as "true." Also, the way the real
teenagers talk about their real lives takes a shape somewhat similar to that
of the two fictional narratives—jumping backwards to memories and forward to hopes and fears, right in the middle of talk about the present. And
the language of all three is colloquial, marked by slang and by "mistakes" in
grammar and usage. My students are careful to include plenty of this slang
and informal usage in their monologues. At the end of the year, when we
stage small-group performances of verbal collages from all the writings
we've read, every group creates as part of its collage a monologue based on
some of the *Times* interviews or the interviews by Robert Coles.

   The article by Anna Kisselgoff, the *Times* veteran dance critic,[6] actually
helped give me the idea for a whole new elective, which I called "Laughter
and Tears." It had to fit into the final trimester—our shortest, only nine
weeks—and I wanted to include art, dance, music, and literature. I also
wanted to address two of my longstanding concerns: (1) that students tend

to find ambivalence in the arts—or in anything—hard to cope with, interpret, or admire, and (2) that by junior and senior year, emotions are stronger than ever, yet kids are encouraged to put away their feelings, deny personal experience, and discipline themselves to focus on a single piece of paper, the college transcript.

So a month ago, by the end of "Laughter and Tears," the juniors and I finished exploring Art Spiegelman's *MAUS,* his powerful cat and mouse "cartoon" narrative in two volumes about how he and his father were shaped by his parents' Holocaust experience; a live performance of Alvin Ailey's classic dance "Revelations," rooted in apocalyptic imagery, spirituals, and jazz, and a video of Paul Taylor's dance "Three Epitaphs" set to a sort of backwoods ragtime; Samuel Beckett's short play *Endgame;* some blues music; Sam Shepard's play *True West;* and Part 1 of Tony Kushner's Broadway hit, *Angels in America.* We began the course with a packet of excerpts I put together: sections from Daniel Goleman's *Emotional Intelligence;* some surrealist poetry; sketches from Monty Python; the graveyard scene from *Hamlet;* a scene from Joseph Heller's *Catch-22;* segments from William Styron's *Darkness Visible,* an account of his clinical depression; Beckett's one-page play "Breath"; critic Martin Esslin's definition of theater of the absurd; humorist Garrison Keillor's account of judging a poetry contest; and the review of Taylor's dances. Our focus throughout was on "reading" the languages of dance, art, music, and language for cues to this complicated matter of tone, complicated especially when the tone oscillated wildly between laughter and tears. We kept a journal for a week on our own emotional swings and mixed feelings. We explored how the body signals our moods and how the body communicates emotion physically, visually, and aurally in dance, theater, and music. We ended the course with fifteen-minute presentations of projects—original dance, jazz, monologues, poetry, scenes, paintings—each of which had to communicate a range of tones along the spectrum of laughter and tears.

Part of the challenge was finding words to analyze the emotional shadings in all these different mediums. Kisselgoff's dance review was particularly helpful because it offered us language that could be used in talking and writing about tone not only in dance but in other art forms as well. As we read the article, I asked each person to form two columns of words, one for the "tears" and one for the "laughter." One student's "tears" column included: *angst, poignant, acerbic, vibrato, hypocrisy, pathos, sepia, mope, sinister, plague, darkness, disturbing, infection, jarring, ragtime, vulnerable, tension, blind, distortion, golden glow, weighted movement.* Her "laughter" column included *poignant, acerbic, hypocrisy, parody, ragtime, mincing, gambol, sprightly, devil-may-care, pastoral, romp, exuberant, light, distortion, merriment, relish, slambang, lighthearted, happy, picnic, innocent, acrobats,* and *golden glow.*

"I began to see that certain words could go either way," Alexa explained. "Like *ragtime*—I always thought that was cheerful, upbeat jazz, but the ragtime we heard in the video of 'Three Epitaphs' sounded pretty grim to me, and they said it used to be used for both funerals and weddings."

"Yeah, and now that we've talked about dark humor," said Matt, "I realized that some of the words I'd have thought of as sad really could go on the second column too—so I put *darkness, disturbing, weighted, acerbic, distortion, tension,* and *vulnerable* in both columns."

"And *poignant*—that could go both ways, too," Sandra argued. "You can be pierced by humor, can't you? And *innocent*—that's a really complicated one. I put that in both columns."

"So what determines the emotional color of these words?" I asked.

"She says it right in the article—wait a minute, right here," and Alexa read: "'The two pieces have an underlying Taylor preoccupation with light and shade.' . . . No, that's not it, here—'for all their exuberance, they never blur the meaning of the jarring subtext that Mr. Taylor injects into the surface merriment'—No, it's further on—here, it's about the dance that gets performed twice each show with different lighting and weight: 'much of the "context is everything" idea relates to the changes in Jennifer Tipton's nuanced lighting, which can grow astonishingly sinister, as well as to the change in cast. It all depends on the context.'"

"Yes, and when I saw this dance, 'Polaris,' live, I got the same feeling. It took me a while to realize it was the same dance being performed all over again, the second time, but by the end it did feel different. I just couldn't figure out why. Now I'd like to see it again. She says the music has more vibrato the second time, and the different dancers who do the second round add weight to the movements and land 'emphatically on the beat' of the music, that there's a sense of 'angst,' and the golden lighting creates a feeling of vulnerability. But the other two pieces convey 'light and shade' in different ways, simultaneously. And that word you read, *subtext,* refers to a contrasting tone that lies under the surface—*sub,* as in *subterranean, subliminal, subconscious.* And the piece called 'Dust,' with those images of the plague and blindness spreading, is complicated by the choice of music—the 'happy, pastoral harpsichord sound' of a piece called 'Concert Champetre.'"

"You know," said Alexa, who loves dance, "the movements of dancers are more immediate than any words could possibly be. You watch them and your body feels the same tensions and releases and weight and lightness."

"Yeah, but," said one of our poets, "*words* can make you feel tense or light, too. They can be 'poignant' so you really feel pierced. I've read things that made me cry or laugh, and sometimes both almost at the same time."

"I was reading something just the other day that deals with this," I said, "and I think . . . no, I think it was by Stravinsky, you know, the composer who collaborated with Balanchine on a lot of wonderful dances for New York City Ballet. Maybe not—but I *think* it was in the Norton Lectures he gave at Harvard. Well, whoever it was said that no language that tries to describe a work in a *different medium*—words describing a piece of music or a dance, for instance—can possibly do it justice or substitute for the original, though the words of a poem or a novel or a play can be just as powerful as a choreographer's patterns or a composer's harmonies.[7] It's the firsthand versus the secondhand, primary versus secondary. Words can't quite recapture what your body felt when it experienced a live dance piece. But they can help you become more aware of the emotions the dance made you feel. In order to *think* about a dance or piece of music, or a relationship you have with another person, for that matter—I don't mean *feel* on your nerve endings but to make your feelings conscious to yourself and express them— you need words."

## Notes

1. Ludwig Wittgenstein, quoted in Richard Lederer, *The Miracle of Language*, 3 (see note 5, chap. 7)

2. Tom Romano, *Writing with Passion: Life Stories, Multiple Genres* (Portsmouth, NH: Boynton/Cook, 1995), 86–87. Romano supervises student teachers and teaches writing at Utah State University and before this taught high school students for seventeen years. *Writing with Passion* is a beautifully personal book about teaching writing; appropriately for one who pioneered the multigenre research paper, Romano shifts easily between writing exercises and his personal experiences as writer, learner, teacher, father, son, and friend. He alternates chapters on "Truth through Narrative," "Breaking the Rules in

Style," "Melding Fact, Interpretation, and Imagination," and "Dialogue, Poetry, and Song" with his own poems, stories, impressions, and mini-essays. This is a book that makes you pick up a pencil and continue the piece you started at the end of the summer. It begins, invitingly, with Mary Oliver's poem "The Ponds." I can't think of a better way to start a book on writing with passion.

3. Padgett, *Creative Reading,* 81 (see note 2, chap. 8).

4. "Children of the Shadows," a ten-part series, *New York Times*, April 1993. The difficulty with this series is that most of the ten adolescents interviewed are children of color, and those who are living in run-down apartments with a drug-dealing or absentee parent and yielding to the temptations around them reinforce the racial stereotypes that television and films make familiar to students in schools everywhere. Some of the teenagers, however, are shown to be fighting the odds with impressive determination and success. And the series offers good opportunities for discussing the nature of stereotyping and the subjectivity of the media, as well as the role racism plays in wealth and poverty in this country.

5. Robert Coles, *Privileged Ones: The Well-off and the Rich in America*, vol. V of *Children of Crisis* (Boston: Little, Brown, 1977). Child psychologist and author of this five-part series based on his extensive interviews with children of every class and race throughout the United States, Coles in this book focuses on children of very wealthy families, including the grandchild of a mine owner, twins growing up in New Mexico near an Indian reservation, the son of a Florida grower, a Chicana in the San Antonio barrio, and the grandson of a Pullman porter whose father is a successful businessman. Each volume in the series includes drawings made by the children as they talked to Coles and a preface describing the methods he used in gathering his information and impressions. Coles finds striking similarities in the behavior, goals, and anxieties of all these privileged children, and he pictures their particular kinds of suffering with the same understanding he brought to the more obviously oppressed children discussed in his previous volumes. While some of the political issues felt out of date to my current crop of students, they realized that the broader picture was still relevant.

6. Anna Kisselgoff, "When the Same Becomes Very Different," review of Paul Taylor's dances "Polaris," "Company B," and "Dust," *New York Times* (3 March 1997).

7. George Seferis, preface, *Poetics of Music in the Form of Six Lessons* by Igor Stravinsky (Cambridge: Harvard University Press, 1970), ix–x. The Greek poet Seferis quotes Stravinsky as having said, "How misleading are all literary descriptions of musical form," and supports this, as a poet struggling to write about a musician: "Indeed yes, and it is not a question simply of music. Generally, I think, it is misleading to transfer a given artistic expression from the medium which gave birth to it to some other which will, inevitably, be alien." Seferis goes on to cite Mallarmé's poem "L'apres-midi d'un faune," and Debussy's setting of the poem, to make the point that "each art has its own medium, that material which the artist's creative manipulation suddenly and unexpectedly makes more sensitive—molds it into a form different from the way we see it in everyday life." And he ends by marveling at Stravinsky's ability to find words with which to speak about music in his Harvard lectures.

# Chapter 10

# *"Sepulchre or Sealed Honeycomb?"*
# *The Language of Shakespeare*

M ost of us who love Shakespeare want our kids to love his language. It was in pursuit of this desire that I invited a senior boy from the Shakespeare elective into my ninth-grade class to talk about why he had chosen to spend two trimesters with the plays. And while I wish he'd had nicer things to say about *Henry IV, Part 1,* my heart warmed when a ninth grader asked, "Which play did you like best and how come?" and he said unhesitatingly, "*The Tempest*—because the language is so pretty." It's an odd word to hear in the mouth of a seventeen-year-old boy—*pretty*—and may sound a bit reductive when one thinks of Caliban's bitter complaint against Prospero and Miranda: "You taught me language; and my profit on't / Is, I know how to curse: the red plague rid you, / For learning me your language!"—or the drunken joking of Stephano and Trinculo, or Prospero's lofty, moving farewell. But I think John's enthusiasm for a mix of words that to ninth graders reading Shakespeare for the first time seemed like a foreign tongue was as startling as if he'd suddenly fallen into iambic pentameter. Here was a senior they looked up to—a fencer, a stage techie— saying with no trace of embarrassment that words from five hundred years ago were "pretty." He must actually have understood some of those words. Wow!

Before the students and I start reading *Othello* together, I hand out a sheet of Shakespeare's curses (ranging in intensity from "Forsooth" and "thou knave" to "a Pox on thee" and "'Zounds" and "'Sblood," followed by explanations where necessary), along with some choice insults (e.g., "thou cream-faced loon") and a few handy, oft-used forms and expressions ("Prithee," "he hath" and "thou dost," "ere" and "e'en," "in sooth," etc.) We try them out in brief improvisations: I give each small group a plot outline of one of the first three scenes of act 1 and ask them to assign roles and improvise this bit of plot for us in their own colloquial English but slipping in as much of the sixteenth-century lingo as possible. The result is usually appalling, but the confusion and silliness make a start at dispelling Bard-fear. The students get the sounds of the words in their mouths and the actions in their bodies, and they begin to learn the names of the characters. Then we read the first few pages of the play aloud to hear how Shakespeare set up the opening situation and how he used the language. All this makes the first reading assignment a little less daunting.

I give the class a second preliminary assignment, one that grew out of my reading Richard Lederer's *Miracle of Language,* specifically his piece about Shakespeare's language: "A Man of Fire-New Words."[1] Lederer asserts that Shakespeare was "the greatest wordmaker who ever lived." And he goes on to cite statistics:

> Ongoing research demonstrates that there are 20,138 lemata (dictionary headwords) in Shakespeare's published works. That figure represents approximately forty percent of the total recorded for the English language up to the year 1623—and Shakespeare could not have owned any dictionary in which he could have looked up these words! For purposes of comparison bear in mind that the written vocabulary of Homer totals approximately nine thousand words, of the King James Bible eight thousand, and of Milton ten thousand.
>
> Of the 20,138 basewords that Shakespeare employs in his plays, sonnets, and other poems, his is the first known use of over 1,700 of them. The most verbally innovative of our authors and our all-time champion neologizer, Shakespeare made up more than 8.5 percent of his written vocabulary. Reading his works is like witnessing the birth of language itself.

And then Lederer, quoting Prospero's lines to Caliban—"I pitied thee, / Took pains to make thee speak. I endow'd thy purposes / With words that made them known"—goes on to compare Shakespeare to Prospero: "he dressed our thoughts with words and teemed our tongue with phrases." Next comes a wonderful list of compounds and "double plays" that Shakespeare seems to have invented. These include "proud-pied April, heaven-kissing hill, and world-without-end hour," as well as "barefaced, civil tongue, cold comfort, eyesore, faint-hearted, fancy free, foregone conclusion, foul play (and fair play), half-cocked, . . . laughing-stock, leapfrog, lie low, primrose path, sea change, stony-hearted, tongue-tied, towering passion, and yeoman's service."

I give this list to my students, along with quotations from Lederer's article. I ask them to read the invented words aloud and circle their favorites. We talk a little about some of these—about what they mean; about the power of figurative speech and the yoking of concrete and abstract; about how compact the metaphors are; about Shakespeare's ear for different sorts of music and his apparent interest in every kind of world, from the outdoors of oceans and woods and gardens and stars, to the law courts, to the church, to the government, to children's games. We also discuss which words are already familiar—perhaps even clichés by now. "Could a cliché ever be resurrected, made fresh?" I ask. They're not sure. I suggest that humor writers get good mileage from clichés—S. J. Perelman, P. G. Wodehouse, Dave Barry. And that a cliché used in a new context can take on a whole new life. Then I ask them to create some descriptive compounds of their own that are effective as figurative language, as sound and image, and to write definitions for them.

Next day most of them are eager to show off. We get:

> *sapmouthed*—i.e., sapmouthed fool, whose words stick in his mouth like sap—adj.
>
> *fire-tongue*—one who's always lashing out—n.
>
> *ear-itch*—the desire to hear what you want to hear—n.
>
> *marshmallow-hearted*—someone who has a hang-up with movies like *Sleepless in Seattle* or *You've Got Mail*—adj.
>
> *verbal feces*—useless or untruthful speaking, garbage talk—n.
>
> *cloud-feet*—light tread; "She was walking on cloud-feet in the early morning"—n.
>
> *mind-bumped*—bewildered, dumbfounded—adj.
>
> *batterbeat*—the kind of noise which tears at one's insides until it has full control and respect—n.
>
> *cloud-puncturing sun*—a sun so bright it punches through clouds—adj.

*barren-eyed*—having eyes that don't convey anything—adj.

*sinpriest*—one who, though outwardly righteous, is inwardly full of pain and whose soul is tarnished by sin—n.

*trickster angel*—someone who plays good tricks—n.

*foggy yapper*—one who talks on and on but never says anything clearly—n.

*fluffhead*—head not made of fluff but thinking like fluff—n.

*memory burner*—an object that burns memories into one's heart or soul—n.

*heart-dedicated*—completely in love—adj.

*nose-attack*—the obligatory action at a sad event, such as any movie with Julia Roberts, meaning you have to wipe your nose just to fit in, pretending you are sad like everyone else—n.

These students were beginning to get excited about word making and about the use of figurative language to characterize people and situations. Maybe they were ready to look closely at how Shakespeare used images and sounds to create different language for different characters. I also wanted them to start imagining from the sounds and images a character uses how he might move and dress. I wanted this to happen before the kids began tangling with the entire play, so I excerpted four speeches, two by Iago, one by Othello, and one by Cassio, for reading aloud and close analysis. I hoped they would be able to recognize the similarity between Othello's and Cassio's language in contrast to Iago's, and then, later, as we moved through the play, that they would notice how Othello begins speaking in Iago's images and rhythms—how his thoughts are manipulated by Iago. I made a point of choosing one of Iago's prose passages and one of his irregular, fragmented iambic pentameter speeches and contrasted both of these with two smooth-metered speeches of Othello's and Cassio's from early in the play, when Othello comes safely through the storm to be reunited with Desdemona on the isle of Cyprus.

I asked the students to answer a set of eight questions and write up a final description about all four speeches:

1. Is it prose or poetry? How can you tell?
2. What categories or "worlds" do the images come from? Cite examples. (Most of the students recognize that Cassio's and Othello's speeches are full of sea imagery, that Iago's speeches draw on animals, food, body parts.)
3. Which kinds of sentences dominate the speech: statements, questions, commands, or exclamations?
4. Would you say the speech flows smoothly, in terms of punctuation and line breaks, or is it broken up a lot? (Read it aloud again.)

5. Are the lines noticeably weighed down or slowed down by polysyllabic words—say, words of three or more syllables? Do you notice a lot of short words, and if so, what effect do they have? Give examples.

6. Is there a notable quantity of concrete nouns? Or do abstract nouns seem to dominate? Or is there a balance? Give examples.

7. Do particular patterns of vowel or consonant sounds dominate the speech? Plosives, dentals, liquids, nasals, sibilants? Long vowels or short? What effect do these patterns have? (Keep reading aloud.)

8. Are there any allusions to religion? Cite examples.

9. Taking all the above observations into account, describe briefly your impression of each of these three speakers—intention, frame of mind, ethics and values; how you imagine each might move on stage; what kind of costume you'd picture each one wearing—colors, cut, fabrics, props.

As I look back on some of the answers I saved from this past year's crop, I notice how, typically, individuals brought their own temperaments and experiences to their readings. Brian, responding to Othello's speech on his reunion with Desdemona, noted,

> More dark words—death, die, fear, unknown fate—some commas but still very flowing but sudden bursts of exclamations, the death words really make a statement, an eerie feeling, the only religious allusions are "as low as Hell's from Heaven"—I think the speaker is probably going to die.

Tom comments,

> Othello proclaiming his joy, declaring his love and what he would go through to be with Desdemona . . . a lot of one-syllable words which makes it go fast, he can't stop himself . . . made up almost entirely of words that convey his love, "May the winds blow till they have wakened death," the winds are literal and figurative—no feat of nature can dampen his love, but they also represent any other obstacle their love may encounter. . . . I see Othello as wearing flowing, colorful robes, a grand, maybe haughty man who has a dramatic, romantic side. I imagine his movements to be graceful and smooth. . . . I can't imagine him being underhanded or sneaky like Iago. . . . He seems like a victim, soppy and gullible type that'll fall for anything.

("Soppy"—Not surprisingly, this is the boy who created the two compound words attacking sentimentality in the movies!)

I warn the students that this assignment—given over two nights—will take more time than they might think but that it will pay off in the long run. It will prepare them to read the play at a level of interest, feeling, and understanding that may surprise them. And, in fact, it does. In our later discussions, students turn to language—to metaphor and rhythms—to make their cases. When we watch video clips from various productions, they have definite opinions about directorial choices, about costume design, about actors' interpretations. When they choose a passage to memorize and perform, most of them have some favorites. When we work with Laban energy movements, they are quick to associate "wring" or "press," "flick" or "float," with specific characters at particular moments in the play. We view José Limón's modern dance piece "The Moor's Pavane," which is based on the relationships of the two couples, Othello and Desdemona, Emilia and Iago, and students are able discuss the pros and cons of dance versus words as modes of exploring emotions and story. Their final papers quote the language of the play, not only to support a point about plot but also to investigate issues of aesthetics and emotional truth.

Despite all this preparation, around the middle of the play I always worry that everyone is still rooting for Iago. They think Othello is an idiot to distrust Desdemona and Cassio on such little evidence and not to see through Iago's dishonesty. They find Iago much more interesting, and they don't seem able to empathize with Othello's suffering. They don't see much potential for tragedy. It's usually at this point that I trot out the freewrites they did on jealousy before we started the play so that we can revisit their appreciation of what this emotion feels like.

We started this freewrite with a free-association exercise: "Let's take five minutes right now to try some 'streamy' writing. When I say to start, you'll write the word I give you and then just let the pencil go on writing whatever it wants till you hear me say 'Stop.' Don't worry about whether you're writing sense or nonsense. Don't stop to think. The pencil has to keep moving—it can write the same word over and over till it comes up with something else. You're responsible for nothing except keeping the pencil moving. No right or wrong, and you don't have to show me or anyone else what ends up on the page. Close your eyes for a moment. Shake out your wrists. Listen to your breathing. . . . Okay, write 'jealousy.'"

If they've done this kind of activity before, I can usually write along with them. If not, I circulate quietly, pushing a hand that has stopped writing, maybe offering some images to keep pencils moving: "You're a skater gliding over the ice, nothing gets in your way, you're a horse running smoothly, your mane flowing out behind you. . . ."

"Stop. Now, read over whatever you can make out of what you've written, listening and imagining. Circle any combination of words that interests you, that sparks a thought or picture of jealousy. Maybe you won't find anything this first time. Letting your unconscious go free takes practice." I read them my own page:

> jealous whiteworm mire gravegravid steam sandroller sandworms
> jealous empire memorycrunch mirror self silver selfmade mercury
> silverfish roach rising deep crawl depthcharge jelous gelid icycold
> chilly friend tongue blue swollen hate want many towers sidewalk
> icy minaret point sharp prick finger witch spin gold jealous heart
> ache wish wish wish whisk under bed conceal paintover drown lake
> treasure you guard can't give up want keep lock chest ache ake ach
> alas grows swells grave under grass mound gas swell corpse
> stonebury press down; burn self capital J curve cross top stich pin
> prick thimble.

Then a few students volunteer word combinations. We make a list of the images they offer, and we explore possible associations with jealousy, including physical sensations: why so many images of tightness and coils, of underground and slime, of suffocation, of pricking?

I ask them to try a forty-minute freewrite at home that night on the concept of jealousy. They can start with another five-minute "stream" if they want, or move straight into the informal journal-style writing that I call freewriting, in which one thought or experience may be followed rather randomly by another—in which they don't have to worry about organization and are allowed to write fragments and run-ons as long as they stick with the single topic. They can draw on their own experience; on jealousy they've read about or heard about; on song lyrics, movies, paintings; on the sound of the word; on its derivation, its synonyms; on how the feeling begins, builds, ends; on its physical manifestations; on whether it has any positive side; and so on.

Next morning, students volunteer to read sections (or, if time is short, I collect everyone's and photocopy anonymous excerpts for the following day). Tom wrote:

> We are always jealous of someone, something. At times it gnaws at
> our insides like nothing else, at others we convince ourselves that
> we aren't really jealous at all (which is a lie). . . . I actually do
> experience a physical reaction to jealousy. It's almost like a surge of
> adrenaline; the jealousy will boil inside of me until, in a final push,
> my face flushes just for a second, and then subsides. I'm safe until
> the next time. . . . Jealousy has been dangerous for me, but not in
> the ways that one might expect. The danger in jealousy for me
> doesn't exist as a ball of rage, but rather as an ultra-compressed ball
> of repressed rage. I'm confident I'll be able to keep it down, but that
> is where the problem lies. Keeping it down, playing it off has
> become so routine that it's unhealthy. I don't think I've ever had a
> jealous rage, which I think is probably unusual. So the danger is, if I
> have one, will I be able to control it?

Many features of this piece remind me of the different stages of
Othello's experience, including the "gnawing" image and the need to deny
the emotion entirely. Ian came up with the image of poison—which Iago
and Othello both use—and also, unbeknownst to him, expressed Othello's
pain at "not being what you should be." He captured some of the tragic
sense of loss that Shakespeare wrote about:

> You have to be able to admit to yourself what you can barely stand
> to admit; . . . you feel badly about yourself. . . . Jealousy is when
> you feel that you can't be what you should be, and you feel that
> someone else has succeeded where you have failed. It's really
> horrible. . . . I think that nobody can stay jealous for too long
> because it would be unbearable. If you need to lie to yourself about
> something, I think that you really need to tell the truth. . . . I think
> there is much truth to the phrase "jealous rage." . . . Anger can
> really be poisonous when you are jealous of somebody. . . . You
> really envy them but dislike yourself. When you feel this way . . . it
> can lead to things being said and done that you really don't want to
> do. Then you become even more frustrated and angry because you
> think that what you did to this person will make you feel better, and
> when it doesn't you feel more frustrated. . . . [Y]ou are still jealous
> and you *still* haven't gotten what you wanted.

Emelia's freewrite paved the way for us to discuss Othello's inexperience with love and with white women. (He listens carefully to Iago's explanations of "supersubtle Venetian" women and tells himself that Iago may well be right, since he himself knows little about them.) "People seem to feel jealousy in situations where they feel uncertain or threatened by their surroundings." She also noted that "words can harm the human mind so badly that friends do not recover."

Katie wrote, in contrast to those students who worried about their need to repress feelings:

> Jealousy consumes you. . . . I think lower of myself in every aspect, not just the one someone is currently better than me in. This in turn leads to a sudden bad mood or depression. . . . I avoid the envied person. Then eventually we collide and a fight ensues. We usually talk into the wee hours of the night and bare our souls and cry a lot. This takes place in about a day. (A very nerve-wracking day.) . . . When jealousy takes over and threatens to destroy your relationships, it's a problem. I don't really try to prevent it, because I *like* to yell at Meredith late at night. I like to let her know how I feel and I always hope that next time she won't pay more attention to guys than to me. She never changes. Neither do I. And so the late-night arguments continue.

This student concluded with the thought that "[m]ost people in the competitive society we live in today are very familiar with jealousy. People who are removed from everything and set their own standards are really better off. They have no reason to see themselves as worthless in any way." This observation suggested to me that Othello's separateness from the Venetian society up until he fell in love with Desdemona might have helped him "set his own standards" and be the confident, independent figure he is in the first act of the play.

I learn a lot about my students from this kind of writing, in which they feel free to explore their feelings and aren't preoccupied with sentence structure and word choice. In some cases, they write better—mechanics included—when they are this relaxed. Each year some of them cite certain freewrites when asked to name which of their writings they liked best. I was interested to see that most of the boys wrote about repressing their jealousy (or said they rarely felt jealous), while most of the girls wrote about "talking it out."

But this particular assignment on jealousy also helped them enter into the emotions of both Othello and Iago. When we returned to these freewrites in midplay, they understood better the torment Othello was experiencing and where it might lead. And we were able to take a closer look at Iago's possible motivations: how much did jealousy of Cassio and Othello contribute to his plotting? To his scorn? We looked at his speeches about the degree to which man can control his passions; was he in as much control of his emotions as he implied? Did he act purely from "motiveless malignity"?

I've learned one exercise with Shakespeare's language that I haven't yet tried with ninth graders, but I want to. It's worked well with eleventh graders. I call it the Macbeth Symphony.

> To-morrow, and to-morrow, and to-morrow
> Creeps in this petty pace from day to day
> To the last syllable of recorded time,
> And all our yesterdays have lighted fools
> The way to dusty death. Out, out, brief candle!
> Life's but a walking shadow, a poor player
> That struts and frets his hour upon the stage
> And then is heard no more. It is a tale
> Told by an idiot, full of sound and fury,
> Signifying nothing.

I was at Lincoln Center Institute in New York where a group of teachers were being prepared by a theater director to see *Macbeth* and, later, to help prepare their students to see it. David, the teaching artist, a professional director and actor, recited the famous soliloquy twice. Then, rather than analyzing its imagery or the character's state of mind or the "beats"—shifts of mood or intent within the speech—he asked each of us to choose one or two of the words we'd heard. We were to explore the sound and "feel" of the word until we came up with a way to say it that satisfied us. He wasn't any more specific than that, but a warm-up exercise paved the way for us to think about words in terms of their music.

He asked us to say our names to the group in several different ways and then helped us analyze the musical techniques we'd used—shortening and extending the duration of a sound; varying the accents, which altered the rhythm; repeating one of the syllables; using a variety of pitches for the different syllables; increasing or decreasing the volume; attacking each syllable (making it staccato) or smoothing the sounds out (legato); changing the timbre or color (by saying the name through the nose, for example, or gargling it). So we knew that we could apply any of these techniques to our chosen word from the Shakespeare text.

But since we'd heard the word in the context of this soliloquy, our treatment of it was likely to reflect the speech's emotion in some way, as well as associations we might have with the word. By the time everyone had chosen, most of the key words and phrases in the speech had been covered and some by more than one person. Each of us went off into a corner of the stage and experimented till finally we were called back together to present our words. David went around the circle, listening to each person so that he would know what repertoire of sounds he had to work with. Then he explained that he would conduct us, and demonstrated a few simple signals by which he'd indicate when he wanted someone to enter, to cut off the sound, to repeat it, to get louder or softer, to speed up or slow down.

He started us with the person who had chosen "no more"—and we heard repeated two little, high-pitched sighs of words, almost as brief as water drops. Then a man's voice joined in with the same phrase but his version was drawn out and in a much lower register, giving a spectral, doom-ridden effect. "Tomorrow" entered—a third layer, though David soon cut off the others and gave it a solo. With the "morr" softly accented and extended so that it sounded like "mar," it suggested the slow, hopeless creeping of time toward its "last syllable." "Out" entered on a high note that made almost two syllables of the "ou," so it sounded like the wail of an animal in pain. "Last syllable" was whispered, as if time had run out of breath; the hiss of the two s's had a ghostly effect. "Brief" was a high, descending note, plangent, helpless, futile.

Then several of us took turns conducting. We introduced the words and phrases in a different order, experimenting with shifts in volume and tempo and contrasting various layers of sound to solos. Obviously, this was not what we would be hearing on stage at the performance, but the experience of listening to the all-too-familiar lines fragmented and layered in this way gave the language new life for us. We had it now in our bodies, in our throats, on our lips, and in our ears, and this heightened the emotional power of the words.

As I ponder this experience, I remember how Kathleen Norris, in *Cloister Walk*, speculates on the power of participating in plainsong in the Benedictine monastery. She writes:

> Like so many elements of monastic life, Gregorian [chant] is a matter of focus. It teaches us what we gain when we become simple, dependent upon the beauty of the unadorned human voice. It teaches us what we lose, in music, when we add a melody and a beat. It fosters an appreciation for community. Gregorian can't be sung alone.[2]

We twenty teachers certainly weren't *singing* Shakespeare. We were twenty very "unadorned" human voices, creating something without melody or beat, but I think we felt ourselves becoming a community, focused by the power of Shakespeare's sounds and images coming together in a totally unpredictable and mysteriously meaningful way.

I tried the exercise with the students in my Shakespeare elective—a group of juniors and seniors—warming them up first, since they were self-conscious about making unusual sounds in front of one another. Even before playing the name game, I got them all moving in a big circle to relax and then asked each student to call him- or herself to dinner—in whatever voice, words, and intonation the student was used to hearing. Some of the boys' imitations of their mothers definitely broke the ice. Then I helped them produce and analyze variations on the sounds of their names. Finally, we moved on to Macbeth's soliloquy.

Of course, the lines weren't as familiar to the class as they had been to the English teachers in New York. It wasn't so much a matter of having to make them hear the language freshly; it was more the need to get them off the page so they could really listen for the *first* time. But once again, this unconventional method of working with the sounds of the phrases, of breaking down the meaning-on-the-page and taking sounds into our mouths and ears, had the effect of physicalizing and heightening the emotions of the speech. One student said later, "Wow! When I read this the first time, I just felt, the guy's a murderer, you know? But now I'm sorry for him. And I started to think about what it would be like to feel this way about your life. And how Shakespeare knew. . . ."

## Notes

1. Lederer, *The Miracle of Language,* 93–101 (see note 5, chap. 7).

2. Norris, *The Cloister Walk,* 330 (see note 2, chap. 2).

# Chapter 11

# "The Inward Eye"

**W**hen you pressed your nose to the window as a child, maybe hoping for snow, or counting raindrops, or breathing on the glass in order to draw something with one finger, you were on the threshold of the outdoor world. You could just push up the glass and the screen and stick your head out. And if you gazed long enough, letting your mind travel outward, it might bring back some new understanding of itself in words. Words that you wrote down or maybe just thought to yourself. Words mediating between self and other. Richard Lewis, who works with children as a writer in the schools, says in his *Living by Wonder*:

> She [a child looking silently at an exhibit of photographs] touched the part of me that is at the core of our learning: the solitude of ourselves speaking with ourselves. We might legitimately ask, where is the solitary part? Is it located in a place within our minds to which we retreat when realities press too strongly against us? Is it accessible at all times, or is it available only when certain conditions allow it to exist? How do we know that solitude exists in us at all?

And in answer, he suggests:

> To immerse ourselves in the existence of something other than ourselves often enables us to touch and express the inner world. . . .

> To teach toward our solitude is to use the experience of solitude as a
> synthesis of our complex world, a mediating point out of which a
> personal clarity can eventually emerge. To find an expression from
> solitude is to find a language through which we can hear our-
> selves—and listen to others."[1]

That last sentence interests me particularly—the mysterious process of
finding a language that lets you hear both your own voice and those of
others. I look out the window. . . .

Peck-cheep. Two small brown birds are spearing breadcrumbs with their
beaks. Everything is small—the crumbs, which they peck into still smaller
fragments. The cheeping sounds. The tips of their beaks and the little
quiver as their necks jerk forward in quest of food. I'm surprised to see each
bird take a turn passing a crumb deftly from its beak to the other's. A cloud
blots out the sun for a moment, and I imagine the feathered panic, the small
ruckus that might occur if that darkness took the shape of a hawk's wing. Or
would they even notice in their minute concentration on the crumbs?

How is what I see through the window calling up these words? How is
my mind registering what I'm seeing? Smallness seems to be the controlling
idea, captured in words—*fragments, cheep, tips, little quiver, minute, crumb.*
My mind seeks out categories to contain what it's seeing. The metaphor of
"spearing" crumbs—this is what the beak action translated into, somewhere
even before it got onto the page. Those short *i* sounds that seem to have
clustered, instinctively, around the birds' smallness—*tip, quiver, little, panic.*
And *feathered panic*—the mind juxtaposing words from two different realms.
How did *jerk* rise obligingly into consciousness as I watched the necks
move? And *deftly*—I remember thinking *meticulous,* but, almost unconsciously, effortlessly, shifting to something smaller, more physical, more
birdlike and less like a human intention. And what about the imagination's
quick journey from the actual dark cloud I saw to the possibility of a hawk
flying overhead: the mind's readiness to flit from the present scene to
something remembered, some knowledge it already has, and to project an
"if." The birds' concentration struck me as a physical thing—the intensity of
their search and their beak action, the accuracy in passing crumbs to one
another. Even that, intense as it was, I found myself thinking of as "minute."
How much concentration, after all, can a bird's brain and body exert?

My body and mind seemed to work together with what I was seeing and
what I already "knew" in order to register it in words and, at the same time,

respond to it—again, in words. I was seeing and hearing with the mind's eye and ear, touching with "the mind's hand," categorizing, remembering, imagining, all in words.

It's interesting that so many books on writing ask us to consciously "search" for "the best words" in order to describe something, rather than describe something in order to find the best words.

The next day I find myself returning to my journal record on the two birds. I write, quickly, with irritable crossings out:

*These two brown
birds are very
small, and so are
their sounds
as they pinpoint
crumbs, peck-cheep,
they seem too
small for anger,
where could it
lodge in that con-
centrated quiver?
They can't be
parent and child,
they exchange
crumbs, passing the
daily bread from
beak to beak.*

*If I were that
small, would my
anger shrink to
pinpoint? Fit
my horny beak,
peck-cheep, take
that, and that!
I would not
give up, I'd stuff
my small bird's
craw with wrath,*

*I would probably*
*starve to death,*
*or forget to watch*
*for the hawk's*
*shadow, I'd be*
*so lost in the*
*pounding heart*
*of my own*
*small darkness.*

I realize as I write that I've been thinking for the past three days off and on, especially late at night—it was keeping me awake—about how angry I still am with a particular friend, how at times when I couldn't sleep I wanted this anger to disappear, while in actuality I knew I didn't feel ready for that to happen. These feelings are coloring the way I am writing about the birds today. The way the two things coalesce in words as I write is helping me clarify my feelings. For the first time, I realize, I'm able to laugh a little at my anger—self-critical laughter, resentful laughter, maybe, but still. . . .

I also remember that just before I looked out the window and saw the birds, I'd been reading a poem by James Wright in which St. Jerome, late into his desert life of monasticism, experiences a moment of revelation as he looks into the blazing gold, the "deep place," in a lizard's eye. He experiences this moment of joy without having been consciously praying or "beating his breast" over Christ's suffering on the cross or the human suffering in the world. At first he doesn't even see the lizard—he thinks it's a fallen branch.[2]

How much had the words of the poem "prepared" me to find revelation in two brown birds?

I had been almost entirely alone for two weeks in residence at an artists' colony in the Canadian Rockies. My studio, an old fishing boat come to rest at the foot of the mountains, had been my home for ten hours a day, with no interruptions except the squirrels and birds who came to my windowsill for crumbs—and the movement of my own mind and the people locked inside it. What role had this solitude played in "synthesizing the complex world," in offering "a mediating point for personal clarity," in "finding a language in which I could hear myself and listen to others?"

In *Living by Wonder*, Richard Lewis talks of how he tries, in the schools he visits, to "teach toward our solitude." I think it's important to help create an *understanding* of solitude so that students will have a chance to find this synthesizing, mediating language. This experience is just as important for high school students as it is for the young children Lewis is writing about, but for adolescents it can be more difficult to achieve, in both practical and psychological terms. And for many teachers and schools, making a place in the curriculum where such a mysterious-sounding language can have mastery seems equally difficult.

One day the juniors and I were reading Wordsworth's poem about the daffodils: "I Wandered Lonely as a Cloud." A student brought up the closing lines about the inward eye being the bliss of solitude: "I don't think solitude's all that great," she said. "And I bet writers don't either. They probably wish they were at a cafe with their friends. Or even at the mall."

"Well, speaking personally as a struggling writer," I said, "solitude's pretty blissful—except when the writing's not going well. Solitude is when and where I can hear my mind talking to me. But I know it sounds like a typically romantic word. And probably the various synonyms for it sound even worse. Let's collect some."

And soon we had written on the board: *solitude, alone, lonely, lonesome, apart, separate, segregated, isolated, remote, withdrawn, introspective.*

"Let's rank them from 'worst' to 'best,'" I suggested. "We can look them up in the dictionary later—it sometimes has mini-essays of a few sentences on shades of difference among synonyms—but for now, just rely on your gut reactions."

Most students placed *apart* or *separate* or *solitude* at the top of the list and *lonesome* or *segregated* at the bottom. "What associations—connotations—do you think affected your rankings?" I asked. No one could quite explain why *lonesome* appeared at the end of his or her list. "It just sounds so sad." So we checked the dictionary, and sure enough—"depressed or sad because of the lack of friends or companionship" was the first definition. But *lonely* was also defined this way—as "affected with or causing a depressing feeling of being alone; destitute of sympathetic or friendly companionship, support, etc.: a lonely exile." "So in the end," I suggested, "it comes down to a slight difference in sounds—maybe the way that 'some' echoes 'lone' and the way the *m* extends the word, making it hard to get over."

Some students connected *solitary* with solitary confinement, and many associated *separate* with divorce. Most of us thought of racism when we heard *segregated*, though one student argued that there might be times when segregation was a positive thing: "like if you choose to segregate yourself from hostile people, or if healthy people are segregated from contagious ones." And when we looked up the word, we found not only "to require, often with force, the separation of (a specific racial, religious, or other group) from the body of society," but also "any kind of setting apart, forced or natural, including the separating of certain genes during meiosis."

Some of us heard in *apart* certain melancholy lines from songs about broken romances, and a few associated the word with *apartheid.* Others thought of *apartment,* and here the association varied; for some students, getting their own apartment was a positive idea, a sign of independence they looked forward to, while for others who lived in an apartment with their families and wished for the privacy and spaciousness of a house, the word had negative connotations. Then there was Julie, who said, "I think of those apartments in Brooklyn, rundown and full of roaches, that are always burning down and being reported on the news."

*Isolated* and *remote* struck many as more neutral—a matter of being geographically or spatially apart from others but not necessarily being emotionally isolated; one could live in an isolated or remote part of the country and still have friends. There was always e-mail. A few remembered isolationism, from history class, but that seemed too remote to stir any feelings one way or the other. Someone mentioned isolation cells. The students had never heard of *remote* being used about a person's temperament or state of mind. *Withdrawn* seemed to many to refer to a deliberate choice, though some saw it as negative quality, an unattractive standoffishness or even a sign of instability or clinical depression. The dictionary gave us first the neutral "removed from circulation, contact, competition, etc." and then "shy, introverted."

"Let's try to figure out how much the *sounds* of the words affect your feelings about them. Read them over silently, but moving your lips and listening. Notice how each word feels in your mouth." There are times when lip movement during silent reading is actually beneficial. Poet Ron Padgett makes a good case for subvocalizing—hearing in your head each word on the page—as a means of hearing the writer's voice.[3]

Most of us were struck by the effect of the *l*'s and long *o*'s—the mournful sound they made together: *lonesome, lonely, alone, isolated.* The sounds of *apart, separate,* and *segregated* sounded crisper, less emotional. The effect of the *o* in *remote* was lessened by the sharp *t* that cut if off. I quoted from Coleridge's "Rime of the Ancient Mariner" the lines that describe the mariner's sense of spiritual and psychological isolation after he's shot the albatross and all two hundred members of the crew fall dead around him:

> Alone, alone, all, all alone
> Alone on a wide, wide sea!
> And never a saint took pity on
> My soul in agony.

"Listen to how Coleridge is working with the sounds of *alone*—not just those *l*'s and *o*'s but the long, repeated cry of the *i* in *wide* and the way *soul* picks up the sound of 'alone, alone.' But on the other hand, here's Wordsworth praising *solitude* for granting him the power of 'the inward eye.' One kind of separation seems to make possible a deep communion with nature, while another is agonizing punishment. Let's look up just those two words—*alone* and *solitude*."

We found that *alone* came into the language in the 1200s in the form of the Middle English *al one,* meaning "all (wholly) one." Its current meanings include separate, apart, or isolated from others; to the exclusion of all others; unequaled, unexcelled; solitarily, or by oneself; without aid or help (The baby can stand alone). None of these definitions seemed necessarily negative; "unexcelled," as in "alone among his peers in artistry," was, in fact, positive. Yet many in the class thought instinctively of feeling alone or being alone as a depressing state rather than as being set apart because of one's superior talents. And even the latter possibility struck some students as a negative: "Because if you're the best at something, people get jealous, even your friends, or they think you must be conceited, and pretty soon you really do feel alone."

"And does that ever make you hold back from getting really good at something?" I asked. "Do you dislike people who try hard to make team captain or get the highest grades or the lead in the play? Does standing out—for whatever reason—result in loneliness?"

"Maybe, but in the end it's worth it," one girl said. "Survival of the fittest is a good thing." Which is where a lot of our discussions seem to end up. I pointed out how easy it is to accept social Darwinism when we don't actually have to watch "the less fit" being wiped out—when they are as faceless to us as some unknown species of seaweed that failed to make it into the twentieth century. And I thought about some lines I'd recently copied into my notebook from Bertolt Brecht's "I, the Survivor":

> *I know of course: it's simply luck*
> *That I've survived so many friends. But last night in a dream*
> *I heard those friends say of me: "Survival of the fittest"*
> *And I hated myself.*[4]

There was a pause—silence can be a good thing and we shouldn't always rush to fill it—and we went on with our research. *Solitude* came to the English language around 1300 from the Latin *solus*—sole, only. Its definitions include the state of being or living alone, seclusion; remoteness from habitations; a lonely, unfrequented place. *Solitary*, on the other hand, in one of its definitions specifies deliberate choice—avoiding the society of others— and offers as illustration "a solitary cabin in the woods."

"So when and where do you *like* the feel of solitude?" I asked. "Let's write for maybe fifteen minutes—half the time on this question and half the time on when and where you *hate* being alone. Listen to yourself, and see what you find out. Let's start by closing our eyes—here, I'll shut the blinds and turn out the lights, too—and picturing places where we've experienced solitude. See what feelings come back. And what images and words you associate with the positives and negatives. Remember the E. E. Cummings poem where he weaves together the letters for 'loneliness' and 'a leaf falls'?"

It turned out that for many students, solitude was their own room with their own music (and in some cases their own telephone and computer). They looked forward all day to the moment when they could disappear into this sanctuary. And those who had to share a room with a sibling either pulled rank or sought privacy elsewhere. I'd written about how at summer camp I used to escape to a certain rock by the lake at the very borders of the camp land, and how much I looked forward to the Sunday night chamber music concerts, when I could sit on the porch overlooking the lake and lose myself in the music. "Did anybody find they like feeling alone in the midst of a crowd?" I asked.

A few students said yes, they liked how their minds could be alone, could wander anywhere, even if they were sitting in a room with people they didn't relate to, or maybe in a course they didn't like.

"I wrote a whole poem in religion class," said Ilona.

"But that's not real solitude," somebody else said. "It's better when you're alone in the woods or in, like, a cafe, some place where you can watch the people—where you know you won't be interrupted for a while."

"So would you go to a rock concert alone?" I asked. They looked at me as though I were insane.

"When you're enjoying solitude," I asked, "do you find yourself more likely to daydream? Or maybe to start remembering moments from the past? Did anybody write about that?" Yes. And how that kind of mood led them sometimes into writing, or improvising on the guitar, or painting.

"You have to be in the mood," said one girl, "and when there're other people around, you get distracted. But if I had to be alone like that all the time, I'd hate it. You need the balance. I think even writers need to be with people sometimes. How else would they get stuff to write about?"

"Yes, and in fact," I told them, "although Wordsworth pictures himself at the beginning of the poem wandering 'lonely as a cloud,' he was on a walk with his sister Dorothy when he saw the daffodils. Her description of them in her journal even gave him some of the language for his poem, though he needed 'solitude' in order for his 'inward eye,' his imagination, to fuse with the initial experience and create the poem. Notice his image of the 'flash'— the sudden, transient light that brings back the daffodils in all their blowing brightness? *Flash* seems to be the word that helps him bring to consciousness what the moment of recollection is like. The word lets him know his own experience, as well as tell you about it. Did any of you find specific images turning up as you wrote about solitude?"

As some of the students wrote or drew their images on the "open journal" on the wall, I noticed that some were producing pictures of windows. The kids agreed that a window says both positive and negative things about solitude. "It separates you from what's outside, and even the view you get from it is limited by the frame, but that can be good."

"Yeah, you can concentrate on just this little world, take it into your mind and see what happens in there. And if you get bored with yourself, or with what's inside the room, there's always that other view."

"You can open the window to get sounds and smells or even call to somebody out there on the other side. You're inside *and* outside. You're alone and you're not alone."

Their discussion reminded me of a book I'd been reading, *Nine Gates: Entering the Mind of Poetry*, in which the poet Jane Hirshfield talks about *liminality*—from the Latin word for "threshold." She says that writers need to find a way to live in "a threshold state of ambiguity, openness," a "state of being 'betwixt and between'" that enables them to see beyond conventional assumptions about language, people, self, and society, and to be "permeable," able to connect to everything and everyone. This is a state which enters the consciousness through "language awake to its own connections—language that hears itself and what is around it. . . . It begins . . . in the body and mind of concentration."[5] Her words made me think of Richard Lewis's description of solitude giving expression to itself in "a language through which we can hear ourselves—and listen to others," a synthesizing of "this complex world, a mediating point out of which a personal clarity can eventually emerge."[6]

Lewis is not speaking of professional writers, but of all children and the adolescents and adults they will become. He worries that "many children have become unsure of their ability to use language for their own feelings and thoughts" because schools believe this imaginative language is "a special kind of intelligence, the property only of 'gifted' children."[7] Hirshfield takes his concern a step further: "In a culture that likes to think it is founded on the powers of logical, rational mind, the term 'imaginary' has taken on overtones of the trivial or frivolous."[8]

I thought back to my experience with the two birds outside the window, the way the mind discovers words to synthesize observation and response, self and other. I thought about how eager adolescents are to engage with "the real world," how intensely they feel, and how much I want my students to experience in their own minds the language that brings these two things together. Hirshfield says, "In writing lit by a liminal consciousness, the most common words take on the sheen of treasure—transformed into meaning for the entire community because they have been dipped in the mind of openness and connection."[9]

Next day, Sapna hands me a poem she has written called "A Walk in the Woods":

> *A step back*
> *from the world*
> *into            the            world*
>
> *like a Zen Buddhist*
> *Koan*
> *of sweet strawberries*

when facing death
coming back
Life.

a tree breaking
in the woods
slow,        crreeaaakk

unaware of time
a pond appears
from the mists       of       nowhere

and ducks fly up
to touch the sky
as the trees

getting taller and taller
reach
like hands

while the trickles
of calm creeks
lead to a small field

where the wheat
sways in the breeze
which rustles the leaves.

I sit in the sun
with eyes closed
my body aware of     every     breath

emotions rise and I ask
what has come?
gone?

There are green pines
growing in the woods.

> *Do they care*
>          *about*
>                    *my*
>                              *life?*

I know Sapna has been reading Wordsworth and a lot of Gary Snyder. But she also seems to be finding her own solitude and with it a language that synthesizes inner and outer. Her words are common—not "difficult" enough for a test. She hasn't had to struggle to master them. They have found their way to her, taken mastery over her. She is hearing and writing words that have taken on the sheen of treasure, having been dipped in the mind of openness and connection.

## Notes

1. Lewis, *Living by Wonder,* 75–79 (see note 6, chap. 3).

2. James Wright, "Jerome in Solitude," in *The Journey,* quoted by Jane Hirshfield in *Nine Gates: Entering the Mind of Poetry* (New York: HarperCollins, 1997), 171–72. Jane Hirshfield, a poet and translator of Japanese women poets and a longtime student of Zen Buddhism, quotes and comments on Wright's poem in her chapter "Facing the Lion: The Way of Shadow and Light in Some Twentieth-Century Poems." This is the most thought-provoking and inspiring book I have read about poetry, language, and learning; Hirshfield's responses to poetry exemplify how an attentiveness to sound and image enable one to learn about the nature of the spiritual simply by reading a poem. Since the book is hard to describe, I can't do better than quote poet Gary Snyder:

> It takes nerve to talk about "nine gates." Jane Hirshfield, for all her mild tone, has a diamond-hard set of insights to share and no fooling. Her territory reaches from ancient Greece to traditional Japan, from the preliterate to the refinements of contemporary literacy, and she sews them together. These expansive, fearless essays are on the basics of—not poesy in any small sense—but mind, wit, stalking, silky focus, the eros of knowledge, the steely etiquette of art.

3. Padgett, *Creative Reading,* 111 (see note 2, chap. 8).

4. Bertolt Brecht, "I, the Survivor," in *Poems 1913–1956,* ed. John Willett and Ralph Manheim (London: Methuen, 1976), 392.

5. Hirshfield, *Nine Gates,* 203–4 and 3.

6. Lewis, *Living by Wonder,* 79.

7. Lewis, *Living by Wonder,* 119.

8. Hirshfield, *Nine Gates,* 184

9. Hirshfield, *Nine Gates,* 209.

# Appendix

I realize now that I must have written *Dancing with Words* partly out of a vague sense that I hadn't seen many books by teachers on this kind of dance. Visiting the language section of my public library, I found primarily dictionaries, books of a semiscientific or rather speculative nature on how sounds are made and how alphabets and syntax evolved, books on how to prepare for standardized tests and how to teach English as a second language, and a few lively and/or curmudgeonly attacks on the rapid decay of English-as-we-knew-it. A rather motley crew. My own list of suggested books is also motley—a strange mix of approaches to the pleasures of words, some the practical experiences of writers in classrooms, some the musings of interdisciplinary minds on everything from how such a mind makes language to how an ancient Chinese poem should be translated. At least three of the books focus on the art of translation, a process that forces us to examine the musics of word and metaphor more intensely than we normally would. Some of the books offer games and exercises; as a writer, I naturally play with words, but as a teacher I need frequent reminding to do so. There must be other books out there that should be on this list. If you have recommendations, I would welcome them.

BOOTH, ERIC. *THE EVERYDAY WORK OF ART: HOW ARTISTIC EXPERIENCE CAN TRANSFORM YOUR LIFE*. NAPERVILLE, IL: SOURCEBOOKS, 1997. This is a thoughtful and passionate study of the process of making art and its role in daily living. Booth, an actor and arts educator currently on the faculty of the Juilliard School and formerly on the staff of the Lincoln Center Institute, has useful things to say about words, etymologies, and metaphor and their place in the creative life as he draws connections among the literary, visual, and performing arts in "making and reading the world." He reminds us that etymologically the verb "to read" meant to advise, to inform, to interpret, and that "reading the world" requires us to perceive, assimilate, and use. Booth cites an interest in etymology as an example of attending to the everyday as if it were extraordinary—"And then it is." "I attend to the words I use as if they were good stories. A word catches my attention, and I dig into its history. . . . Indeed, for me, this particular habit has prompted some of the deepest world-making of my life."

BURKE, JIM. *THE ENGLISH TEACHER'S COMPANION: A COMPLETE GUIDE TO CLASSROOM, CURRICULUM, AND THE PROFESSION.* PORTSMOUTH, NH: BOYNTON/COOK, 1999. Chapter 3 in this helpful compendium treats "the place and purpose of vocabulary instruction," starting with an epigraph from Voltaire: "Language is very difficult to put into words." Burke admits to having found few references to teaching vocabulary in the professional books most commonly used by English teachers, and summarizes the existing research concisely: read, read, read. But he offers some arguments in favor of special instruction in vocabulary, and describes some good activities, particularly several involving semantic mapping or analysis of words. He also notes the political implications of *not* helping students acquire the knowledge of language that "grants them access to the larger world of ideas and power." And he recommends Princeton Review's *Word Smart: Building an Educated Vocabulary* as a source of word roots, suffixes, and prefixes.

GASS, WILLIAM H. *READING RILKE: REFLECTIONS ON THE PROBLEMS OF TRANSLATION.* NEW YORK: ALFRED A. KNOPF, 1999. Few activities make one more aware of the subtle distinctions between closely related words than the translating of poetry. In the course of exploring Rilke's character and work, Gass compares passages from his own translation of the *Duino Elegies* to versions by many other poets and scholars, enabling us to appreciate the challenges confronting the translator.

GOODING, MEL, ED. *A BOOK OF SURREALIST GAMES: INCLUDING THE SURREALIST DICTIONARY.* BOSTON: SHAMBALA, 1991. This collection of games invented and played by Breton, Magritte, Ernst, and others invites us into the world of surrealist play that "is more like a kind of provocative magic, in that it breaks the thread of discursive thought" and "produces results ranging from the hilarious to the mysterious and profound."

HOFSTADTER, DOUGLAS R. *LE TON BEAU DE MAROT: IN PRAISE OF THE MUSIC OF LANGUAGE*. NEW YORK: BASIC BOOKS, 1997. This is a large, quirky, personal, and imaginatively structured book, best for summer vacation reading, though also fun to dip into at any time. Author of *Gödel, Escher, Bach*, Hofstadter is a professor of cognitive science at Indiana University, where he teaches in the comparative literature, computer science, psychology, and philosophy departments. He directs the Center for Research on Concepts and Cognition, studying the mechanisms of analogy and creativity. *Le ton beau de Marot* helps us listen to language as it presents eighty-eight diverse translations of a short poem in rhymed couplets of three-syllable lines by a witty sixteenth-century French poet, Clément Marot. Some of the translations are by Hofstadter, who became obsessed with the challenge ten years earlier, and others are by family members and poet and scholar friends. Along the way, we hear how Hofstadter fell in love with French and Italian and music, and we get his views on other linguistic experiments, including Daniel Halpern's edition of *The Inferno* as translated by numerous contemporary poets. Throughout, Hofstadter explores the workings of the creative mind and the nature of love and loss—specifically of his own beloved wife, who died before the book was completed. The book begins, "Picture Holden Caulfield all grown up, now a university professor, writing a book about translation. Okay, don't. It's too silly."

NAGY, WILLIAM E. *TEACHING VOCABULARY TO IMPROVE READING COMPREHENSION*. URBANA, IL: ERIC CLEARINGHOUSE ON READING AND COMMUNICATION SKILLS/NATIONAL COUNCIL OF TEACHERS OF ENGLISH, AND NEWARK, DE: INTERNATIONAL READING ASSOCIATION, 1988. Nagy, a senior scientist at the Center for the Study of Reading, University of Illinois at Urbana-Champaign, cites various studies that show that many widely used methods of vocabulary instruction (such as requiring students to look up, define, and memorize definitions or guess meanings from contexts) fail to increase reading comprehension, often because they don't produce in-depth word knowledge. Powerful approaches require "integration, repetition, and meaningful use." This practical and imaginative booklet offers a helpful range of approaches that lead students to engage actively and thoughtfully with words. Nagy also reminds us that readers can tolerate a certain proportion of unknown words in a text, roughly 15 percent, without their comprehension being disrupted, and that, happily, the proportion of unfamiliar words a reader normally encounters is likely to be lower than this. And he reinforces what we all know— that "regular, extensive reading can supply all the characteristics of powerful vocabulary instruction." In fact, if students could read, in and out of school, fifty minutes a day "in high quality, appropriate texts," they could learn four thousand new words a year without any special instruction at all. Intensive teaching "is most appropriate for words . . . representing complex concepts that are not part of students' everyday experience" but that one wants them to incorporate into their writing or speaking vocabularies. The words should be "important to the understanding of a reading selection or because of their general utility in the language," and they are best presented in clusters that relate to a single topic. Perhaps Nagy's most important advice is not to let prereading activities, including vocabulary work, steal too much time from reading itself.

ORWELL, GEORGE. "POLITICS AND THE ENGLISH LANGUAGE," IN *THE COLLECTED ESSAYS, JOURNALISM, AND LETTERS OF GEORGE ORWELL*, VOL. 4. NEW YORK: HARCOURT BRACE & JOVANOVICH, 1968. This article contains what is still one of the best short checklists against bad writing, especially its final item, "Break any of these rules sooner than say anything outright barbarous." It's also a convincing demonstration of how thought can corrupt language and how language can also corrupt thought.

PEI, MARIO. *THE STORY OF LANGUAGE.* REV. ED. NEW YORK: NEW AMERICAN LIBRARY, 1984. Pei, an Italian immigrant who taught languages in New York City high schools and colleges for many years, wrote this book in the 1940s. Some of the etymologies are apparently inaccurate, but the sweep of the book is exuberant, with chapters about many different languages and their histories; sections on language's relation to science, religion, family, politics, economics, etc.; and a final chapter on the need for a universal language.

PINKER, STEVEN. *THE LANGUAGE INSTINCT.* NEW YORK: WILLIAM MORROW, 1994. Director of the Center for Cognitive Neuroscience at MIT, Pinker has focused on language acquisition in children, but his interests are wide ranging, as are the areas from which he draws his analogies and examples. (Woody Allen and Monty Python turn up in the index.) This book is a study of language as a human instinct, wired into our brains by evolution. I particularly like the chapter on "Language Organs and Grammar Genes," which concludes with a prediction that in different people some connection between language circuitry and the intellect or emotions might be faster or slower, thus producing "the raconteur, the punster, the accidental poet, the sweet-talker, the rapier-like wit, the sesquipedalian, the word-juggler, the owner of the gift of gab, the Reverend Spooner," etc. There follows a page of excerpts from Yogi Berra, Dr. Seuss, Vladimir Nabokov, Martin Luther King, Jr., and Shakespeare.

PINKER, STEVEN. *WORDS AND RULES: THE INGREDIENTS OF LANGUAGE*. NEW YORK: BASIC BOOKS, 1999. This is another lively book, extending and qualifying Noam Chomsky's theories by arguing that language consists not only of a mental grammar of creative rules but also of a mental dictionary of memorized words (including irregular verbs).

ROBINSON, SANDRA R., WITH LINDSAY MCAULIFFE. *ORIGINS*: VOL. 1, *BRINGING WORDS TO LIFE*, VOL. 2, *THE WORD FAMILIES*. NEW YORK: TEACHERS & WRITERS COLLABORATIVE, 1989. These two volumes together offer a practical and imaginative way to engage students with the origins of words through studying word families and using the words in creative writing. They include a concise history of the English language, as well as poetry examples ranging from traditional African to twentiety-century American sources and poems using imagery of relevant word families. The preface is by Calvert Watkins of Harvard University.

SEARS, PETER. *SECRET WRITING: KEYS TO THE MYSTERIES OF READING AND WRITING*. NEW YORK: TEACHERS & WRITERS COLLABORATIVE, 1986. Beginning with a game of hangman, this imaginative collection of two hundred thinking and writing exercises, which includes Sears's own responses as he writes along with the students, is designed to help teenagers at all levels of ability take a fresh approach to acquiring and using language by experiencing firsthand "the way language is made." There's a chapter on creating code, as Chaucer and Lewis Carroll did; one on breaking conventions effectively (in the good company of E. E. Cummings); one on inventing words and using what you've invented; one on the language of numbers; another on traffic signs, cattle brands, and Egyptian hieroglyphics; and a final chapter on sending messages into space. Sears has taught high school English and creative writing as well as participated in writers-in-the-schools programs.

SPERLING, SUSAN KELZ. *POPLOLLIES AND BELLIBONES: A CELEBRATION OF LOST WORDS*. NEW YORK: CLARKSON N. POTTER, 1977. This book offers an irresistible collection of words that faded out of the language three or four hundred years ago, each defined and annotated and presented in Sperling's own dialogues, verses, and stories. Glop too much bellytimber and you risk becoming a porknell.

WEINBERGER, ELIOT, AND OCTAVIO PAZ. *NINETEEN WAYS OF LOOKING AT WANG WEI: HOW A CHINESE POEM IS TRANSLATED*. MOUNT KISCO, NY: MOYER BELL, 1987. What happens when a four-line Chinese poem from twelve hundred years ago is translated into

English, Spanish, or French? This little book gives us the poem in its original Chinese ideograms, then in a transliteration, then in a character-by-character translation, and finally in sixteen different translations, each followed by Weinberger's critical commentary. As Paz notes, Wang Wei's poem is particularly resistant because it "carries to an extreme the characteristics of Chinese poetry: universality, impersonality, absence of time, absence of subject. . . . [T]he solitude of the mountain is so great that not even the poet himself is present."

WOOLDRIDGE, SUSAN G. *POEMCRAZY: FREEING YOUR LIFE WITH WORDS*. NEW YORK: THREE RIVERS PRESS, 1997. A writer who works for California Poets in the Schools and also leads adult workshops, Wooldridge focuses on how to "drop a line into the pool of words around you and within you to begin making poems that express more than words can say." This is one of those books that makes you want to pick up a pencil and start writing with your students.

ZAVATSKY, BILL, AND RON PADGETT, EDS. *THE WHOLE WORD CATALOGUE 2*. NEW YORK: TEACHERS & WRITERS COLLABORATIVE, 1977. A stimulating collection of ideas for word games, writing, visual arts, drama, and music by writers-in-the-schools, this book includes essays about creativity in the classroom, bibliographies of books and records, and work by children. It recognizes, as Phillip Lopate says in his article "The Transition from Speech to Writing," that "words can have a visual, totemic power, in addition to, or sometimes even opposed to, their utilitarian meaning, which arrests the reader in his flight" (pp. 24–25), and it offers many ways to help students tap into this power.

ZINSSER, WILLIAM. *ON WRITING WELL: AN INFORMAL GUIDE TO WRITING NONFICTION*. 4TH ED. NEW YORK: HARPERCOLLINS, 1990. Zinsser's lively discussions of style and audience are useful for both teachers and students as reminders of the practical reasons for choosing words with imagination and care.

# Author

Judith Rowe Michaels, author of *Risking Intensity: Reading and Writing Poetry with High School Students,* serves as Artist-in-Residence, K–12, at Princeton Day School and is a poet in the schools for the Geraldine R. Dodge Foundation. Michaels, who earned a Ph.D. in English from Bryn Mawr College, has published poems in many journals, including *Poetry, Yankee, Poetry Northwest, Columbia Review,* and the *Women's Review of Books.* In 1995 she won a New Jersey State Council on the Arts Fellowship in Poetry. She was a consultant on teacher outreach for PBS's poetry series with Bill Moyers, *The Langage of Life,* as well as for the satellite broadcast from the 1998 Dodge Poetry Festival and Moyers's 1999 series *Fooling with Words.* She has served as a writer and consultant on arts education for the Lincoln Center Institute in New York and for Young Audiences of New Jersey, and gives poetry workshops around the country. Michaels's first collection of poems, *The Forest of Wild Hands,* which focuses on her mother's and her own experiences with cancer and draws from her teaching experience, was published in May 2001. Readers interested in Michaels's books can check her Web site at judymichaels.com, which includes audio readings, notice of upcoming presentations, and links to her publishers and to various cancer Web sites.

*Dancing with Words*

Composed by Electronic Imaging in Veljovic and ExPonto.

Typeface used on the cover is Triplex.

Calligraphy by Barbara Yale-Read.

Printed by IPC Communications on 60-lb. Lynx Opaque Offset.